Those Ugly Emotions

This book is a guide to managing negative feelings and using them constructively to develop a closer relationship with the Lord. While psychologically sound, it is not a psychology book; rather, it stresses the role of the Word of God in living our lives.

Those Ugly Emotions

How to manage your emotions

Ken M. Campbell

Christian Focus

Ken M Campbell is an Associate Professor of Biblical Studies at Belhaven College in Jackson, Mississippi. A native of Scotland, he has pastored churches in the UK and in the USA. He is married and has one daughter. He holds degrees from the University of Aberdeen, Scotland (MA), Westminster Theological Seminary, Philadelphia (BD, ThM), and the University of Manchester, England (PhD).

ISBN 1-85792-244-1

First published in 1996 and reprinted in 2001 by Christian Focus Publications, Geanies House, Fearn, Ross-shire, IV20 1TW, Great Britain

www.christianfocus.com

Cover design by Owen Daily

To
The members of
Covenant Presbyterian Church
Rochester, N.Y.,
in memory of six years of fellowship and service together

Acknowledgements

Several friends and colleagues have given me helpful suggestions and comments on this book, and I would like to acknowledge in particular the kindness of Bruce Bezaire, Rich Walters, Jay Adams, Jim Hurley, Corinne Livesay, Nancy Whetstone, and Cille Norman. The responsibility for the remaining faults and inadequacies is entirely mine.

Contents

Foreword

It is a pleasure to commend the new book by Dr. Campbell entitled *Those Ugly Emotions*. It is a book in which the author endeavours to help the reader manage what he calls 'negative emotions'. Clearly, all our emotions are from God; in and of themselves they are not negative. However, because of human sin, emotions may be aroused for the wrong reasons, released in the wrong ways, etc. Emotions become 'negative', i.e. harmful to others and to the one who exhibits them, under such circumstances. Thus, the need for this book. Rightly, the book points out that the current emphasis on 'following feelings' is dangerous. One must evaluate and handle those emotions according to the Scriptures, the Word of God. In his book, Ken shows us how to do so.

The Psalm are filled with the emotional experiences of God's saints. They, pre-eminently, guide us in the way in which God expects us to deal with seven emotions: fear, depression, anger, guilt, hatred, envy and jealousy, and grief. The book is filled with anecdotal material which helps illustrate the points that are made. Perhaps the greatest benefit is in the way in which one learns to *use* the Psalms in meeting many experiences in life.

It is my hope that the book will do much good in helping confused, upset saints. Dr. Campbell is to be commended for dealing with this all-important matter.

Jay Adams
Enoree,
South Carolina

Introduction

Do you feel guilty when you experience negative emotions? Do your feelings ever cause you to do something you strongly regret? Does conflict rage between your beliefs and your emotions? Do your feelings get in the way of your growth in holiness?

If so, cheer up—you are perfectly normal!

Understanding our negative emotions and knowing what to do about them has always been a problem for Christians as well as for unbelievers. Christians cannot accept some current ideas about emotions, such as 'if it feels good, do it'. We cannot go along with the new age theology that tells us that feelings are always good, are at least neutral, and so we should 'follow our feelings'. The solution to negative emotions is not 'getting in touch with the inner child', whatever that means. Nor can we accept the notion that knowledge and insight come from the instincts rather than from the mind. On the basis of the Word of God (not to mention our own experience), we know that our emotions are affected by sin just as much as our minds and bodies.

On the other hand, we do not wish to go to the opposite extreme and assert that all human emotions are intrinsically evil; feelings are no more evil than the mind or the body. But like the mind and the body, human feelings can

11

be the occasion of sin. Emotions can be and often are the root that bears the fruit of sinful actions in our lives. When I use the term 'negative emotions' in this book I mean those emotions which often are the occasion of wrong behavior on our part, but which do not have to be.

But what are we to do? Generally, believers have tended to err in one of two ways. Some have believed that the Christian should suppress his negative feelings, preventing them from surfacing and causing problems. Like the Victorian Englishman, he should 'keep a stiff upper lip'. Such folk usually appear cold and withdrawn and have difficulty with personal relationships. The other extreme is to just 'let it out'. Since feelings are 'only natural', they should be openly and fully expressed. Once you vent them, you can carry on with your life as before. Such people are often unaware of the hurt they cause to others by the unrestrained expression of their negative emotions.

The Psalms of the Old Testament, most of which are about human emotions, offer us a third way to manage our emotions; one that is more effective than either of the above and actively helps us to grow in our knowledge of God. The Psalms present no magic solutions or quick fixes, but they do offer the prospect of steady growth in spiritual maturity. In the Psalms we see that our negative feelings are both warnings and opportunities.

Most of the psalms are about human emotions. John Calvin said that all human emotions are described in the Old Testament psalms: 'There is not an emotion of which anyone can be conscious that is not here represented as in a mirror. Or rather, the Holy Spirit has here drawn to the life, all the griefs, sorrows, fears, doubts, hopes, cares, perplexities, in short, all distracting emotions with which the minds of men are wont to be agitated.'

God graciously gave us the Psalms to help us deal wisely with our own emotions. Even some therapists who do not regard the Bible as the written Word of God often use psalms to help 'disturbed' people, because they are so realistic and encouraging.

The humanist thinking that permeates our society claims that our feelings are good and reliable. If it feels good to you, go with it, follow your feelings, feelings cannot be wrong. This is a serious mistake. Some emotions are harmful to others, and some are also harmful to oneself. The seven emotions discussed in this book that can be harmful are fear, depression, anger, guilt, hatred, envy and jealousy, and grief.

The person who learns and practices the pattern of handling negative feelings that the Psalms offer us will experience the long-term joy that the psalmists knew. This does not come easily, but it is the only way of honoring God with our emotional nature.

My hope is that you will join me in learning to manage our emotions to the benefit of our souls and to the glory of God.

1

Fear

Trembling Soul

Psalm 56

Be merciful to me, O God, for men hotly pursue me;
  all day long they press their attack.
My slanderers pursue me all day long;
  many are attacking me in their pride.

When I am afraid,
  I will trust in you.
In God, whose word I praise,
  In God I trust. I will not be afraid.
  What can mortal man do to me?
All day long they twist my words;
  they are always plotting to harm me.
They conspire, they lurk,
  they watch my steps,
  eager to take my life.

On no account let them escape;
  in your anger, O God, bring down the nations.
Record my lament;
  list my tears on your scroll —
  are they not in your record?

Then my enemies will turn back
   when I call for help.
   By this I will know that God is for me.
In God, whose word I praise,
   in the Lord, whose word I praise—
in God I trust; I will not be afraid.
   What can man do to me?
I am under vows to you, O God;
   I will present my thank-offerings to you.
For you have delivered my soul from death
   and my feet from stumbling,
that I may walk before God
   in the light of life.

Two months after bravely confronting a scissors-wielding store-robber, saving a woman's life and overcoming his own injuries, Don Clendenin was routinely entering his own home with fear-knotted stomach, creeping around his house checking under the beds, in the closets, the bathroom, the back stairs, convinced someone was waiting to jump out at him.

He had entered a pet store two months before to discover a young woman on the floor being stabbed repeatedly by a thief, and instinctively had rushed to her defense. In the ensuing struggle Don was stabbed in the neck, but managed to scare off the intruder. Both he and the lady recovered from surgery, physically fine, but the nightmares would not go away. For the first time in his life Don was fearful and distrustful of people generally. Ten minutes in the past was dominating Don's present and future.

One evening Don's wife Pam said to him: 'Some terrible things happened in those minutes, but now it's time to think about how God figured in them.' They began to talk about the 'coincidences' of that fateful morning: his going to the store instead of his wife going, arriving at the exact moment of the robbery, receiving a wound in his neck one quarter of an inch from his jugular vein yet scaring the man off—all these things in hindsight showed that God had had a purpose for good for all those involved. After seeing himself in the broader purposes of the Lord and realising afresh God's control of all things for the good of His people, Don's fear gradually faded and he was able to get on with his life with confidence.

Psalm 56

1 Samuel 21 gives us the context for Psalm 56, which David later wrote. Imagine you are David. As you are running from Saul, you go to Abimelech, the priest, and ask for food and a weapon. You get a sword, but it is the sword once owned by Goliath! This great sword does not help your situation, because you next flee to Gath in Philistine territory. Since Gath is Goliath's hometown, his relatives and friends might recognize the famous Philistine warrior's sword. In desperation, you pretend to be crazy when you are taken to the Philistine king, Achish, so that you are expelled from the palace. You escape from town and head for the hills, where you discover that one of Saul's servants has been informing on you to Saul.

So here you are, hiding out in caves. The valleys echo with the sound of your pursuers and the threats of what they are going to do to you when they catch you. The Philistines are against you, your own king is against you, you can not trust anyone. You are hungry and exhausted.

How would you feel in this situation?

When I am experiencing great stress, I do not feel like writing songs! But David was a songwriter, and he wrote Psalm 56 to describe his innermost feelings. His dominant emotion was fear, and he cried his eyes out (verses 1-2,5-6,8). At times you may have felt just as afraid as David, perhaps hopelessly afraid. You are an unusual person if you have not. We have all experienced times when it seems that everyone and everything is against us. Even if your imagination has distorted or exaggerated the threat, the feeling of fear is real. Perhaps the fear was not occasioned by the words or actions of other people, but by illness, bereavement, financial reversals. Whatever the circumstance, we have all experienced fear.

What Is Fear?

Fear is an emotion. It is different from worry, though there is a grey area between the two. Worry generally is a mental act in which the mind dwells on difficulties. Fear, on the other hand, is an emotional reaction to imminent danger. Fear is not always bad; God gave us the capacity to fear for good reason. However, since the Fall of Adam in the Garden of Eden, we often fear too much and for the wrong reasons.

Four thousand combat airmen in World War II were quizzed about their feelings prior to a flight. The result of that study showed symptoms that are strikingly similar to those commonly reported during stage fright. In the order of their frequency, here are the top six: (1) a pounding heart; (2) muscular tension; (3) easily irritated, angry, or sore; (4) dryness of mouth; (5) perspiration; (6) butterflies in stomach. [1]

These messages from the brain that cause hormones to be released in the body are designed to prepare us physically to deal with real danger. When airmen in combat experience feelings of fear, it is appropriate and helpful, because they are in a life-threatening situation.

But the same symptoms are less valid for an actress. Her brain is telling her body that she is in imminent dan-

---

1. Jay Adams, *The Christian Counselor's Manual*, (Nutley, Presbyterian and Reformed Publishing Co., 1973).p. 420.

ger, that her life is on the line, but that is not true. Her only danger is the possibility of making a bad impression so that people will think poorly of her. That is vanity.

When a preacher feels the same emotion and has the same symptoms, he is afraid of what people will think of him, or of his poorly prepared sermon. In his situation fear is not the appropriate response—repentance is. His brain is feeding him wrong information.

Consider a man who has a fear of heights. His brain tells him he will die if he climbs up high, but this information is usually false. His fear is irrational. Of perhaps a woman has a fear of mice or spiders. Her brain tells her they will hurt her terribly in some way. Again this is false information.

In both cases, uncritically accepting false information causes fear. The Hebrew language refers to emotions such as fear with words that refer to parts of the body, such as 'guts' or 'spleen', because we can feel fear inside ourselves. Fear causes a physical sensation. It is a bodily state.

Think of that man who is afraid of heights. One day his house catches fire, and he sees his daughter at a second-story window. How does he react? He gets a ladder, runs up it, and rescues his daughter. What happened to his fear? His body received a stronger more urgent message: rescue the daughter you love! The man does not even think about the height; or if he does, his love overwhelms his fear. The woman who climbs onto a chair and screams at the sight of a little mouse would grab a broom or a candlestick and attack a lion that came into her house. Why? Because she is willing to lose her life to save her children.

This is what John means when he says, 'Perfect love

casts out fear' (1 John 4:18). One way of dealing with fear is to replace it with a stronger emotion—love. About 350 times the Bible tells us, 'Do not fear.' Jesus was never inappropriately afraid. Even in Gethsemane, Jesus felt sorrow and stress, but not fear. Why? Because of His perfect trust in and love for His Father. Even though He knew His Father would abandon Him to condemnation and the pains of hell, He also trusted His Father to raise Him up again.

How can we deal with our fear?

A Pilot's Response to Fear

On April 9, 1992, Phillip Taylor was flying a single passenger in a Cessna airplane to Little Rock, Arkansas. The passenger was a tall, husky man dressed in cowboy clothes who said little until they reached about 2,000 feet. Suddenly Phillip felt the cold steel of a gun barrel against his neck. 'I need this plane,' the man stated, 'I'm taking over.' Taking control of the plane, he ordered Phillip to switch off the two radios and the transponder, preventing air traffic control from getting a fix on the plane, and tied Phillip's arms under his right leg and placed a black bag over his head. In the dark of the bag, Phillip's fear mounted to almost despair; he was convinced the stranger was going to push him out of the plane.

Phillip had always loved flying; he felt as if he was closer to God up in the sky, that he could almost reach out and touch him. Now, he realized, he would find out if God was really close by. 'Dear God,' he prayed, as he recited the 23rd Psalm to himself, 'I'm not in a valley; I'm in the sky. But I am in the shadow of death, and I do fear evil. Please help me.'

As the engine droned, a feeling of peace began to grow inside Phillip, until the stranger beside him asked: 'How do you land a Cessna?' Somehow he talked the man down to the runway of another airport; and to his surprise the stranger ripped the bag from his head, turned to him and commented: 'You're going to have a great story to tell your grandkids. Now get out. And don't look back.'

Now Phillip Taylor is able to confess: 'I'm thankful for every minute ... because 2,000 feet off the ground I did it. I reached out and touched God's hand. And He was there.'

Managing Fear
Solving the problem of fear requires deliberate and careful thought. This thought process involves several stages.

(1) Accept your fear. Accept that this feeling exists – it is real. Do not deny or repress it.

(2) Identify the occasion for your fear. Feelings cannot be wished away; feelings are often involuntary. They are the natural response to messages sent to the body by the brain, which is reacting to perceived danger. Since the message may or may not be accurate, the problem is not the emotion you feel, but the reason you feel it. How real is the danger that causes you to feel afraid?

(3) Interpret the occasion for your fear in the light of God's Word. David interpreted the perceived threat in the context of what Scripture says about God's power, providence and lovingkindness. 'In God whose word I praise, in the LORD, whose word I praise—in God I trust; I will not be afraid' (Psalm 56:10).

God said, 'Be not afraid, for I am with you.' David's fear was redefined by God's Word as occasioned by something not ultimately harmful or dangerous. Though horrible, it was part of life, which is in the control of the Lord.

If you fear death, put even that event in the context of God's promises of resurrection and realize that the sting has been removed from death—there is no longer any basis for fear.

If you fear illness, put it in the context of God's gracious providence, with His enduring purpose of training us to depend on Him rather than on our own resources. It is ultimately not a threat but an opportunity. Suffering is unpleasant; but if God is for us, nothing can separate us from His love. One day our suffering will end as we stand in his glorious presence (Romans 8:18).

If you fear people, ask why. What can they do to you? Kill you? 'Do not be afraid of those who kill the body but cannot kill the soul. Rather be afraid of the One who can destroy both body and soul in hell. Are not two sparrows sold for a penny? Yet not one of them will fall to the ground apart from the will of your Father.... So do not be afraid; you are worth more than many sparrows' (Matthew 10:28-30). The psalmist asked, 'The LORD is my light and my salvation – whom shall I fear?' (Psalm 27:1), and the writer to the Hebrews repeats the message: 'The Lord is my helper; I will not be afraid. What can man do to me?' (Hebrews 13:5,6).

If you fear life because you are a timid person, remind yourself that if God is for you, it does not matter who is against you. Can anything separate you from the love of your sovereign, mighty God? (Romans 8:31-39). Of course not.

Put your fears in the context of the great promises of God's Word and smite the devil with them!

(4) Identify yourself and the God you believe in. When you feel fearful, remind yourself that you are a child of the living God, you belong to Jesus Christ, you have been delivered from sin and bondage, and you are clean and pure and righteous in God's sight. God is the almighty, sovereign, holy, eternal, all-wise God. This great God is your Father. He loves you. He cares for you, protects you, guides you, and loves you passionately and faithfully.

(5) Preach the gospel of Jesus to yourself. The cross of Christ delivered you from hell and is able to deliver you from anything else. You belong to Jesus Christ, your Savior and Lord, who bought you with a price. He will never leave, never forsake you. He will rescue you and will rule over all things for you. He is preparing a place for you and will come back for you.

On December 15, 1989, Pastor Tokes of the Hungarian Reformed Church in Timisoara, Romania, was due to be arrested by the secret police, as so many others had been. When the police arrived with a large van, they found the church surrounded by hundreds of parishioners and believers from other churches. Ordered to disperse, they refused. For two days the crowds remained, holding lighted candles all through the night and blocking the entrance to the church. Before dawn on the 17th, the state police broke down the door and took Pastor Tokes away, battered and bloody. When the crowd did not disperse, the communist forces opened fire and shot hundreds. Still they did not disperse. After 45 years of communist repression these believers had had enough. To the astonishment of the world, by Christmas 1989, President Caucescu and his government had fallen, and Romania was free.

Why did these people suddenly lose their fear after 45 years of living in terror? Because they decided they were ready to die. If a person is ready to die, he will not be afraid of anything.

Jesus said if we want to follow him, we must deny ourselves, take up our cross, and follow him. Are you ready to die for Jesus? If not, you are not ready to live for him. If you are, fear will not be a problem for you.

Believe 1 Corinthians 10:13: 'No temptation has seized you except what is common to man. And God is faithful; He will not let you be tempted beyond what you can bear. But when you are tempted, He will also provide a way out so that you can stand up under it.'

Your Answer to Fear

Jesus Christ is the answer to fear. To know Him, love Him, and follow Him is the ultimate solution to fear. Fix your eyes on Jesus and your fear will wither away. Remember, perfect love casts out fear.

Fear cannot be tackled directly. It can only be overcome by a new feeling that pushes fear out. Elizabeth and
Mary and Zechariah were afraid, but the angel told them
not to be afraid because Jesus Christ would come to be
their Savior and Lord. In the den of lions, Daniel lost his
fear when he became conscious that the Lord was there
too. Let the Lord rule in your heart, so that His perfect
peace and love will defeat your fear feelings.

David said, 'When I am afraid I will trust You, my Lord
and Savior' (Psalm 56:3). David didn't say that when he
was afraid he would go to therapy or repent or go on vacation. In the face of fear, David trusted God. That is a decision we can make. It is an act of faith.

Paul said in 2 Timothy 1:7: God did not give us a spirit
of fear, but a spirit of power, of love, and of self-disci-
pline.' Do you realize what you have? Power, love, and a
sound mind. You have it, so use it. You have the power to
trust and to love. No matter how weak and fearful you are,
His power and love are sufficient. Rely on Him, look to
Him, and laugh at your fears. They will come back, but so
will the grace of King Jesus! Do not be afraid!

Why did God give us the feeling of fear? He gave it to
us for several good reasons — to preserve us from injury,
to develop a reverential attitude to him, and to develop in
us faith and courage. Faith is trusting God against the physical evidence. Courage is doing what your feelings say you
cannot do but God says you can do. Every fearful believer
can, through the power of the indwelling Spirit, become
courageous. We can choose to trust and love God in all
circumstances and experience the meltdown of internal
fear. It may sometimes take time, but it will happen.

2

Depression

How Low Can You Get ?

Psalm 32

Blessed is he
   whose transgressions are forgiven,
   whose sins are covered.

Blessed is the man
   whose sin the LORD does not count against him
   and in whose spirit there is no deceit.

When I kept silent,
   my bones wasted away
   through my groaning all day long.
For day and night
   your hand was heavy upon me;
my strength was sapped
   as in the heat of summer.
Then I acknowledged my sin to you
   and did not cover my iniquity.
I said, "I will confess
   my transgressions to the LORD"—
and you forgave
   the guilt of my sin.
Therefore let everyone who is godly pray to you
   while you may be found;
surely when the mighty waters rise,
   they will not reach him.
You are my hiding place;
   you will protect me from trouble
   and surround me with songs of deliverance.

I will instruct you and teach you in the way you should go;
  I will counsel you and watch over you.
Do not be like the horse or the mule,
  which have no understanding
but must be controlled by bit and bridle,
  or they will not come to you.
Many are the woes of the wicked,
  but the LORD's unfailing love
  surrounds the man who trusts in him.

Rejoice in the LORD and be glad, you righteous;
  sing, all you who are upright in heart!

Gary describes how he sat alone at home, overwhelmed by depression; he was out of work and tired of reading rejections to his job applications. A recovering alcoholic for eight years, he knew that drink was not the solution, and he found his mind wandering more and more to the shotgun in the attic. He records: 'I sank deeper and deeper into despair. My head ached as I fought one black thought after another. Am I losing my mind?' Suddenly a new thought came to Gary: 'Go see Joe'. He had met Joe at AA, an outspoken trucker and farmer, very different from Gary, but who had become his sponsor in AA and who he said was always available to help him.

Driving the three miles to Joe's house, he found Joe in the garage and a warm welcome. For two hours, instead of listening to Gary's problems, Joe told him of the problems he was having, and Gary basically listened. The friends hugged goodbye and Gary drove home, feeling a little better. A week later, Joe stood up at the AA meeting and announced: 'A week ago my life seemed hopeless. In fact I had decided to end it. I picked out a rope and the beam I was going to throw it over. But then, unexpectedly, another recovering alcoholic came by.' Joe looked at Gary, saying, 'God used that alcoholic to save my life.'

The Psalms
Psalm 32 is one of several Old Testament psalms that describe the emotion of depression. Depression is the most common emotional problem. The psychology section in most college libraries has more books on depression than any other human difficulty.

Sometimes a stigma is associated with depression, especially among Christians, who often interpret it as spiritual failure or weak faith. Some are afraid it is a sign of mental illness. Many servants of the Lord who are famous for their godliness and effective Christian ministry also experienced depression: Moses, David, Jeremiah, Elijah, Martin Luther, John Bunyan, C. H. Spurgeon, Amy Carmichael, Hudson Taylor, C. S. Lewis.

Most people will probably experience depression at least once in their lives. God gave us passages in His Word, such as Psalms 6, 13, 22, 38, and 42, to encourage us in times of depression.

Angela was a pastor's wife, very conscious of the unrealistic expectations people had of her. Three weeks before her second child was due, her husband went away on a trip for a few days. There was no expectation of anything important happening in that time. But a couple of days after her husband left, Angela went into labor and gave birth to a baby boy. Three days later when her husband returned home, he found his wife rocking back and forth in a catatonic state; the baby lay on the floor screaming and filthy and Angela was oblivious. Later Angela confided that she had felt depressed after the baby's birth, and had not wanted anyone to see her weeping. Sadly, she was unaware both of the Scriptural comfort that could have helped her, and of a Biblical counsellor who might have helped her through this stressful time; instead she was hospitalized for six weeks.

Our Lord knows our weaknesses. The Great Physician knows how the body, mind and spirit of humans interact, and He has prescribed some remedies for us.

From these psalms we discover the nature, symptoms and causes of depression, and solutions for depression.

Nature of Depression

David does not give a simple definition of depression, and for good reason. Depression is almost impossible to define because it covers such a wide range of feelings. Most people agree generally that depression involves feelings of deep sadness and gloom that affect the mind and the body, as David described in Psalm 32.

A standard textbook of clinical psychology offers five schools of thought on the subject of depression. It then offers ten competing humanist medical models of depression. Recently non-Christian therapists and counselors have been advocating an eclectic approach – dealing with each case on a pragmatic basis using a combination of several different medical models. Following their example, some Christian counselors have tried to define and treat depression without starting from the biblical model of human nature: man is a creature made in the image of God, living (apart from Christ) in bondage to sin's power, but capable of being liberated by the cross through the power of the Holy Spirit.

Non-Christian therapists and counselors cannot fully succeed in treating depression because their medical models of the human condition exclude the spiritual aspect of our being. Depression always has a spiritual dimension. God has given a Counselor, the Holy Spirit, to guide us into the truth of our condition and the solution to it.

The focus of this discussion is not the mood swings

that are a normal part of life. Sometimes these occasional moods have no apparent cause, but often we feel down and unhappy because of some particular event or circumstance in life. This is the favorite theme of blues and Country and Western music because everyone experiences it. This is not a critical problem.

Neither will we focus on the serious condition of clinical depression. Individuals who experience clinical depression may spend a major part of their lives in desperate unhappiness, constantly thinking of death and suicide and unable to function normally. Such a person suffers from a condition caused by something like a tumour in the brain. This person needs medical treatment, as well as biblical counseling.

This chapter does not deal with either of these types of depression. We are talking about an occasional emotional state that is serious, but does not have a physical cause.

Symptoms of Depression

Recognizing the symptoms of depression is easier than defining it. The symptoms are apparent in Psalm 32. In verse 3, the author speaks of being 'silent' before he went to the Lord in confusion (verse 5). He felt physically weak, with his bones feeling heavy and wasting away. He groaned and complained and felt that God was against him. Day and night he found no relief. In verse 6 he refers to a feeling of drowning. This is one experience of depression.

In Psalm 6, the psalmist cries out, 'Be merciful to me, LORD, for I am faint: O LORD, heal me, for my bones are in agony. My soul is in anguish. How long, O LORD, how long?' (verses 2,3). He continues in verses 6 and 7: 'I am worn out with groaning, all night long I flood my bed with weeping and drench my couch with tears. My eyes grow weak with sorrow; they fail because of all my foes.' Here the symptoms include physical aches and pains, exhaustion, sleeplessness, and weeping.

Psalm 13 is similar: 'How long, O LORD? Will you forget me forever? How long will you hide your face from me? How long must I wrestle with my thoughts and every day have sorrow in my heart? How long will my enemy triumph over me?' (verses 1-2). In this situation the symptoms include anguish that borders on despair, internal conflicts in the mind, a feeling of being abandoned by God, and great sorrow of heart.

Psalm 22 is usually understood as describing the state of mind and feelings of our Savior on the cross; indeed He quoted from it as He hung dying. The main feeling here is of being abandoned by God, of being alone and helpless and unable to sleep. The author feels rejected by his fellow-man. He feels surrounded and trapped while physically and emotionally weak and exhausted. Psalms 28 and 42 express this same litany of sorrow, pain and suffering.

William Cowper, an eighteenth-century Christian who wrote many well-known hymns, struggled with depression. Cowper today would probably be diagnosed as having bipolar disorder (or manic depression), and certainly his personal experience of depression goes far beyond what Christians generally experience. Although many of his hymns clearly reflect his faith and hope in a sovereign God, one of the poems he penned describes the sense of hopelessness that a depressed Christian often experiences.

The Lord will happiness divine
On contrite hearts bestow.
Then tell me, gracious God, is mine,
A contrite heart or no?

I hear, but seem to hear in vain
Insensible as steel.
If aught is felt, 'tis only pain,
To find I cannot feel.

Thy saints are comforted, I know,
And love thy house of prayer,
I therefore go where others go
And find no comfort there.

In the first stanza, Cowper expresses his lack of faith; in the second, he expresses his lack of feeling, and in the third, his lack of comfort. These are common feelings in all degrees of depression.

Since everyone is different, our symptoms of depression may not be exactly the same, nevertheless some common feelings are usually evident:

1. Persistent sadness, emptiness.

2. Sense of hopelessness, worthlessness, helplessness.

3. Lack of energy and interest in physical pleasure.

4. Physical weakness, aches and pains.

5. Sleeplessness and difficulty in concentrating.

6. Restlessness and difficulty in making decisions.

7. Unexplained changes in weight.

8. Vague feelings of guilt.

A combination of several or all of these symptoms indicates serious depression.

Panic woke Shella from a deep sleep, and she shook her husband awake crying, 'Please help me.' The darkness had been closing in on her again. She writes: 'I would come home from my job as a medical transcriptionist and collapse into bed without eating. I cried uncontrollably for no reason. I woke up with night terrors. I couldn't make the simplest decisions. Sometimes the smallest task seemed to take superhuman effort.' This unreasonable depression lasted a long time for Shella, even with the support of a remarkably understanding and loving husband.

When she awoke that night, unable to sleep, Will did as he often did; he held his wife close and quietly recited the 23rd Psalm until the truth of its confession and promise broke through her depression and conquered it. He did not complain or accuse her of her frequent failures; he left her alone when she seemed to need solitude; he called regularly to see that she was okay when he was away on a business trip; he would go for short walks with her from time to time to get exercise. Few husbands (or wives) have such wisdom and patience, and Shella is very fortunate (though her husband might have thought to take her to a

Biblical counselor!); but it is the constant reassurance of
the Word of God which got her through the nights.

Occasions for Depression

The occasions for depression are varied and often complex, with many possible factors – physical, mental, spiritual, temperamental, and circumstantial. In his book, *Spiritual Depression—Its Causes and Cure*, D. Martyn Lloyd-
Jones emphasizes the spiritual causes of depression. John
White, in *The Marks of Melancholy*, stresses the physical
causes.[2] Both of these men have medical qualifications
and are biblical in their theology. In writing on the subject
of depression from a biblical viewpoint, they both stress
that attention must be given to spiritual and physical causes
of depression, not one or the other. As White says concerning the works of Lloyd-Jones and the Puritan writer,
William Bridge:

'I must sound a note of warning. To read Bridge and
Lloyd-Jones alone may cause us to assume something
which neither author intended, that all depression is
"spiritual" in the sense that bodily infirmity is never its
source and that it has only "spiritual" remedies. To read
my book with its emphasis on bodily processes may
lead us to err in the opposite direction.'

---

2. D.M. Lloyd-Jones: *Spiritual Depression* (Grand Rapids, Eerdmans,
1965).
John White: *The Masks of Melancholy*: (Downers Grove, IVP, 1982).

Other books on the subject of depression are available. Although many have been written by Christian psychologists, some may be misleading because of a tendency in Christian counseling to adopt non-Christian and even anti-biblical ideas. Few have succeeded in integrating scientific learning about human behavior without also blending the humanist framework of thought with the Biblical paradigm.

In Psalm 32, David describes his cure: 'I said, "I will confess my transgressions to the LORD" – and you forgave the guilt of my sin' (verse 5). Most scholars believe this song was written some time after Psalm 51 and refers to David's sins of adultery and murder. This would be consistent with his statement in verse 3 that he had these symptoms while he was keeping silent, which may have referred to his denial and repression of guilt. His happiness came only when he experienced God's forgiveness again.

David uses three different words in verses 1-2 for sin and three different words for forgiveness, indicating the comprehensive nature of sin and the completeness of forgiveness. In verse 9 he warns us against being as stubborn as he had been, and in verse 10 he encourages us to trust in God's unfailing love. Clearly this particular case of depression was linked to sinful behavior.

Psalm 6 contains no confession of sin, because sin was not the occasion of this bout of depression. The occasion was objective: the overwhelming threat of David's enemies. 'My eyes grow weak with sorrow; they fail because of all my foes. Away from me, all you who do evil, for the LORD has heard my weeping' (verses 7, 8).

In Psalm 13 David's depression was again occasioned

by being surrounded by enemies. He responded with fear, conflict and indecision.

Although sin is sometimes the direct cause of depression, it is not always so. In some cases, depression is a response to genuinely stressful circumstances. In these situations, sin is involved indirectly when we fail to trust in the Lord and overcome our negative feelings with faith and obedience. In 2 Corinthians 4:7-19 Paul argues that no matter how stressful the circumstances, the believer can maintain his spiritual balance no matter how discouraging and painful the situation. Depression does not have to result in sin.

In the case of habitual sins, such as compulsive gambling, homosexual practices, performing abortions, or taking drugs, depression is the direct result of unconfessed sin. But usually other external factors, such as persecution, are involved as well, as David records. Even relatively minor sins such as procrastination can cause depression. Social stresses at work, home, or school put strains on one's ability to cope. It is easy to become depressed.

Perhaps the most common cause of depression is a conflict between objective reality and an individual's beliefs and desires. The so-called 'mid-life crisis' of many men is depression caused by the realization that their career plans are not going to work out. The big house with the big pool and the sports car and the boat are not going to happen: the dreams of being department chair or CEO have gone, and many men do not want to accept a role in life or a position at work that is unrewarding and unimpressive.

Housewives become depressed when household chores

offer little fulfillment, and they long to escape further years of boredom. But career women who believed the feminist promise of fulfillment through independence, singleness, and career success also now write articles about depression. Reality is different from dreams. With a physical basis in PMS and menopause, a woman's depression often has a mixture of physical and spiritual elements due to reacting inappropriately to these circumstances.

Individuals who succumb to addictions are often depressed. Seeking happiness or relief through alcohol, sex, money, drugs, gambling, or food becomes a habit, and the conflict between what is and what should be causes feelings of worthlessness, guilt, and self-contempt.

The first experience of depression in recorded human history is in Genesis 4:3-8. 'On Cain and his offering, God did not look with favor. So Cain was very angry, and his face was downcast.' Cain's depression showed in his face. Why was he depressed? Because he knew rejection, which usually leads to anger and/or depression. The worst rejection of all is rejection by God. The Lord warned Cain that his sins of anger and jealousy would overcome him and become a habit if he did not take vigorous steps to master them. Refusing to listen to the word of God and giving in to depression and unbelief, Cain finally murdered his brother.

Managing Depression

Once again it must be stressed that sometimes depression is due to direct sin, sometimes not. Identifying its source may be difficult. But the refusal to deal with stress in the right way is sin. Then depression may come and the situation gets worse and worse.

As Augustine lay dying, he had this statement put over his bed: 'The beginning of wisdom is to know yourself a sinner.' That is where David began in dealing with depression. He examined his heart for unconfessed sin; after identifying it, he confessed it. When he confessed his sin and trusted in God's forgiveness, the burden of depression was lifted from his heart and was replaced with joy.

But sin was not always the cause of David's depression. At times a conflict between objective reality—the world outside of himself—and his own personal hopes and beliefs precipitated his depression. After recounting his depressing circumstances, David made a commitment: he said, 'But I trust in your unfailing love; my heart rejoices in your salvation. I will sing to the LORD for He has been good to me' (Psalm 13:5-6). He knew that despite everything, he was not an orphan! The Father who loved him was powerful, merciful, good, wise, and trustworthy.

Even our Lord Jesus Christ on the cross briefly expressed desperate feelings of depression due to His abandonment by His Father, but acknowledging His painful feelings, He turned to His Father in faith and trust.

The steps for overcoming depression may be summed up as follows:

1. Identify the cause of your depressed feelings. Is there unconfessed sin your life? Prayerfully examine your recent attitudes, desires and behavior in the light of Scripture and the character of Jesus.

2. If sin is directly involved, confess your sin and believe you are forgiven.

3. If direct sin is not involved, acknowledge your inappropriate feeling of depression; resolve not to follow your feelings but instead believe in God's power to restore the joy of your salvation.

4. Praise the Lord, despite your feelings, for the cross of Christ and for past help and kindness. Remember that you belong to Him in life and death. You are not an orphan.

5. Remind yourself that you are a child of God and God is a gracious, covenant-keeping God of mercy and faithfulness.

6. Remember that the circumstances that provoked your feelings of depression are temporary, and the Lord will take you through them and out the other side, just as He led Israel out of Egypt, through the Red Sea and into the promised land. There is a point to these ugly circumstances: they are to improve your character as you face them together with the Lord Jesus and the power of His Spirit.

7. Exercise your responsibilities: Use God's Word. Read His promises, meditate on them, and pray over them until you really believe them and can rejoice in them by faith.

Eventually, faith will overcome unbelief, and your feelings will change. Even if your circumstances do not change right away, you will know the Lord is taking care of you and you will experience the peace and joy that only He can give.

3

Anger

A Right To Be Angry?

Psalm 37:5-9

Commit your way to the LORD;
   trust in him and he will do this:
He will make your righteousness shine like the dawn,
   The justice of your cause like the noonday sun.

Be still before the LORD and wait patiently for him;
   do not fret when men succeed in their ways,
   when they carry out their wicked schemes.

Refrain from anger and turn from wrath;
   do not fret—it leads only to evil.
For evil men will be cut off,
   But those who hope in the LORD will inherit the land.

Stuart Reininger describes how he lost his temper with his daughter Karen: 'My hand was still tingling from slamming down the telephone. I struggled into my coat and stormed out of my house. I had never hung up on my daughter that way, never cut her off in the middle of a sentence. She deserved it, I thought. She's an inconsiderate kid who thinks only of herself.'

Karen had first postponed an outing with her father from Friday to Saturday, and then called Saturday to postpone their time together again to Sunday so she could be with her friends on Saturday. Certainly such behavior was selfish.

'But even as I kicked the door shut and ran out to the car, I felt a nagging discomfort .... For an instant I thought of going back and calling her to tell her how I felt and to try to make her understand she simply couldn't change plans on a last-minute whim .... then I got into the car. I'd tell her when I got there.'

As he drove along the New Jersey Turnpike the oil-line on his BSA motor-bike (his car wouldn't start) parted, and after he had fixed it the bike toppled over on his leg. His leg snapped and he passed out; gasoline poured out of the tank all over his midsection. Under an underpass he lay in the dark for several hours, invisible to the heavy traffic roaring past. A warm numbness crept over his body, and Stuart realized as he drifted in and out of consciousness that he may easily die there. It was then that he thought how foolish it was to leave his daughter with his angry words as her last memory of him.

'Why did I hang up on her like that?' he agonized. 'God, let me live long enough to tell her how much I love her

and to ask her to forgive me. Don't let her go through life
knowing her father's last words to her were angry ones.'

It was shortly after this prayer that a car stopped where
Stuart lay. Soon he was in the hospital and his fractured
tibia was treated. When he awoke he turned his head to
see Karen standing beside his bed. 'Daddy, I'm so sorry,'
she said. 'No,' replied her father, 'I'm the one who should
be sorry.' And he vowed to himself that he would never
again let the sun go down on his anger (Ephesians 4:26).

According to Francis Bacon, it was Queen Elizabeth I
who said, 'Anger makes dull men witty, but it keeps them
poor.' The playwright John Webster, in *The Duchess of
Malfi*, said, 'There is not in nature a thing that makes a
man so deformed, so beastly, as doth intemperate anger.'

Thomas Fuller, another seventeenth-century writer,
said, 'Anger is one of the sinews of the soul; he that wants
it, hath a maimed mind.' In other words, a person is a
psychological cripple if he is never angry.

Yet most of us are more ashamed of anger than of any
other emotion. Shakespeare said that anger makes fools
of us all. Psalm 37 tells us not to be angry: 'Refrain from
anger and turn from wrath; do not fret – it leads only to
evil.' Is this realistic?

What Is Anger?
Anger is a feeling of displeasure at events in our lives or
at the behavior of others that causes tension and often an
attitude of hostility toward the offender.

In Psalm 37, David first felt irritated, then angry, at the
wickedness of dishonest and evil men. The Lord told David

to control his anger, not because it was wrong in itself, but because in this case it was pointless – the Lord will deal with wicked people in His own time.

Anger in itself is not wrong. In fact it can sometimes be helpful. Anger can arouse courage and master fear to enable a soldier to overcome his enemy or to enable a journalist to expose corruption. Since the Fall of man in the Garden of Eden, however, anger usually is wrong since it is a reaction to opposition to our self-will. If it is not controlled it can lead to hatred, as evidenced by the biblical examples of Cain, Saul, and the Pharisees.

Like all emotions, anger can be constructive or destructive. It is destructive if it harms someone, either ourselves or someone else. It is constructive if it leads us to take action to resolve or improve a situation. If we suppress our anger, we hurt ourselves; if we let it explode, we hurt others.

Symptoms of Anger

There are a half dozen words for anger in the Bible. The basic meaning of one is 'nostrils', because one of the symptoms of anger is the flaring of nostrils! Other physical symptoms are bulging eyes and tightening of muscles, which shows in the face by the tightening of the mouth. Caucasians show anger more clearly than blacks, because their faces may turn red or pale.

Sometimes we clench our fists. Our heart may beat faster and our pulse may rise. Often our voice rises as well, and sometimes that is the first awareness we have that we are in the grip of angry emotion. The symptoms vary somewhat according to our temperaments, and the rate at which people become angry also varies. Sometimes it can be a slow burn, with others it is like a volcanic eruption.

Occasions for Anger

One of the most common occasions for anger is offensive behavior by others, such as cruelty to children. Injustice and oppression can provoke us to anger, but so can nice people who get in our way or interfere with our plans.

Sometimes anger is our response to what someone said or did to us. The playwright Congreve made the famous statement: 'Hell hath no fury like a woman scorned.' Biting comments, name-calling, even a look, can ignite the fires of rage. A girls' gang fight erupted in a high school, with dozens of girls kicking, biting, scratching, pulling hair. After many interviews, the occasion was uncovered: 'She looked at me.'

A person may become angry over the lack of deserved praise from a spouse or gratitude from the children or a promotion at work. There are many occasions for anger, but most stem from interference with our will and desires, which results in pain or insult or threat. We can even become angry with ourselves for doing something wrong or stupid, so that we feel like beating our head against the wall as just punishment for our folly.

Is Anger Right?

Romans 1:18 tells us clearly that God is angry with the wickedness and corruption of mankind. Psalm 7:11 goes further and says that God is angry with the wicked every day. Moses told the Israelites after they made the golden calf that the Lord was angry enough to destroy them (Deuteronomy 9:19).

1 Kings 16:13 informs us that God is provoked to anger by worthless idols. Since God is jealous of His holy name and has a jealous love for His people, idolatry especially arouses His anger, which leads Him to vindicate His righteous nature by punishing the wicked. God hates sin and evil and must punish and destroy it. Judgment day is called the 'day of God's wrath', because He will finally and completely pour out His anger on the devil and all evil.

Thankfully, when God expresses His anger to mankind in history, His anger is temporary and modified by mercy.

Do not confuse the discipline that the Lord metes out to us from time to time as arising from His anger; rather such discipline is the expression of His passionate love to us, a love that is determined to mold us in the image of His Son, a love that uses both blessings and discipline to achieve that goal.

There is an old hymn that says of Jesus, 'No one marked an angry word who ever heard Him speak.' Not so! Scripture recounts several instances in which Jesus expressed anger. He expressed anger against temptation when He said to Simon Peter, 'Get away, Satan!' Jesus Christ expressed anger against the hypocrisy of the Pharisees: 'Woe to you, bunch of snakes!' He voiced His anger against hard hearts (Mark 3:5). Jesus Christ demonstrated His anger against idolatry when He made a whip and drove out the crooked merchants from the temple courtyard, violently pushing over their tables and stools. John says that Jesus was filled with anger (John 2:16-17).

Was Jesus right to be angry? Since He was the sinless Son of God on earth, He was just as right to be angry as was His Father at corruption and evil. But Jesus Christ was never angry because of His own circumstances or His personal situation; He accepted good and bad circumstances as His Father's perfect will for Him. Rather than becoming angry at His potential killers, He felt compassion for them. He literally turned the other cheek when He was attacked and did not strike back. His anger was controlled and channeled constructively to deal with people and problems in an unselfish and righteous way.

If it is right for God the Father and Jesus Christ to be angry, what about us? Do we have a right to be angry? In the Book of Revelation we are told that the Devil is angry because he knows his time is short (12:12). That is self-centered anger, illegitimate anger. May we be legitimately angry?

There are many biblical examples of legitimate anger expressed by God's people, such as Jacob's anger in Genesis 30:1-2, Moses' anger in Numbers 16:14-15, Saul's anger in 1 Samuel 11:16. Samuel, Eliab, Abner, and David all were right to be angry in certain cases. At other times their anger was wrong.

Anger itself is not so much the problem, as what we do with it.

When Anger Is Wrong

Some psychologists and therapists, including some Christian ones, appear to believe that all anger is wrong. They tell Christian parents never to show anger or let their children show anger, but they are mistaken because there is a righteous and legitimate anger. However, anger is usually wrong. No wonder Jay Adams says, 'Sinful anger probably is involved in 90 per cent of all counseling problems,' and he includes secret, unconfessed anger against the Lord.

Anger is wrong when it is directed against a fellow Christian and leads to hostility and a desire to see him punished or humiliated (Matthew 5:21-22). Whenever anger leads to harm or a desire to harm, it is wrong.

Anger that results in a loss of self-control is also wrong (Proverbs 29:11,20,22). Most loss of self-control due to anger occurs in the home. We know that if we vent our anger outside the home – against our boss or against another authority – we will be punished or penalized or discredited. Proverbs tells us that the wise man checks his anger, stopping himself from sinning worse than he already has.

Anger is wrong when it's 'just natural', because our fallen nature is depraved:

'The acts of the sinful nature are obvious: sexual immorality, impurity and debauchery; idolatry and witchcraft; hatred, discord, jealousy, fits of rage, selfish ambition, dissensions, factions and envy' (Galatians 5:19-20).

Fits of rage or loss of temper are fruits of our sinful nature and dishonor creatures who are made in God's image. God's anger is considerate, thoughtful, and purposeful. 'Natural' anger is hasty, self-centered, and foolish.

Anger against God or God's will is obviously wicked when it is nursed and not overcome. 'All who have raged against Him will come to Him and be put to shame' (Isaiah 45:24). Most of us would deny that we are ever angry with God; but if we do, we are deceiving ourselves. Since our sinful nature prefers its own will to His will, when things do not go as we want or expect, our anger, in reality, is directed at God.

Managing Anger
As we attempt to solve the problem of anger, we should follow these guidelines.

1. Recognize the existence of anger and strive to control it. Paul exhorts us, 'In your anger do not sin: do not let the sun go down while you are still angry' (Ephesians 4:26). This means that it is possible to continue to feel anger without giving in to sin.

When the Lord told David to refrain from anger against the wicked (Psalm 37), He meant that David should get control of this feeling rather than giving in to it. The Bible tells us that God is slow to anger, and James tells us to be the same: 'Everyone should be quick to listen, slow to speak, and slow to become angry, for man's anger does not bring about the righteous life that God desires' (James 1:19,20). Paul tells us in Ephesians 4:31: 'Get rid of all bitterness, rage and anger.' We are accountable for overcoming sinful anger by the power of the Holy Spirit.

Proverbs 29:11 also reminds us that anger can be controlled: 'A fool gives vent to his anger, but a wise man keeps himself under control.'

Even pagans understand that they should recognize and control their anger. Horace, who died in 8 BC, said, 'Anger is a brief madness; so control your passion, or it will control you.'

2. We must identify the occasion for our anger. When God saw that the Ninevites had turned from their evil ways, He had compassion and did not bring upon them the destruction He had threatened. 'But Jonah was greatly displeased and became angry. He prayed to the LORD, "O LORD, is this not what I said when I was still at home? That is why I was so quick to flee to Tarshish. I knew that you are a gracious and compassionate God, slow to anger and abounding in love, a God who relents from sending calamity. Now, O LORD, take away my life, for it is better for me to die than to live." But the LORD replied, "Have you any right to be angry?" '(Jonah 4:1-4). That's the question: Is your feeling justified and righteous, or selfish and flowing out of the old sinful nature? Jonah was so angry that he wanted to die, but he was wrong. His anger was a self-righteous anger.

Sometimes other angry people encourage or promote our anger. The Bible says to avoid such people, so that your own anger does not get worse (Proverbs 22:24-25).

We must identify the real cause of our anger, the issue

or the problem – not the person who caused our anger, but the issue raised by that person. Then we can address that issue rather than the person. Even though the person may be responsible for the issue, our intention as Christians regarding that person must be to help him rather than punish him. The issue should be addressed separately.

3. After determining the source of our anger, we must interpret it in the light of God's will. David counsels us in Psalm 37 to see the issues in the perspective of the long-term, the eternal. Remember that God will take care of the wicked eventually – this is not your concern. Whatever the issue may be, put it in the context of God's providence toward you and recognize it as part of His training program for you to learn to trust Him and to submit to His will, whatever the situation is, and to love whoever is the source of this problem in your life.

Our enemies are really not physical, but spiritual (Ephesians 6), and we defeat them by faith in the Holy Spirit and by the use of God's Word and prayer. As we do so, we become able to pray for our enemies and even love them. Love is not easily angered and keeps no record of wrongs (1 Corinthians 13:5).

'Hatred stirs up dissension, but love covers over all wrongs' (Proverbs 10:12). Love and hate are opposites. To prevent anger from developing into hate, anger must be replaced by love. This is only possible by faith in God's grace and power.

4. We must focus our attention on the Lord. We can chan-
nel the energy of anger into physical exercise such as running or swimming, which is a good thing to do in the short-
term. But in the long-term, spiritual exercise is more effective. Spend regular times meditating on God's forgiveness toward you through the cross of Christ, and seek to
experience that forgiveness anew so you can share it with
the source of your anger.

The battle with sinful anger is not easy, but it is possible to win the battle if we train ourselves to recognize and
control the anger God's way; identify its cause; re-inter-
pret it in the light of God's will; and re-focus our attention
on God's undeserved love, kindness, and forgiveness toward us.

4

Guilt

That Guilty Feeling

Psalm 51:1-9

Have mercy on me, O God
    according to your unfailing love;
According to your great compassion
    blot out my transgressions.
Wash away all my iniquity
    and cleanse me from my sin.

For I know my transgressions,
    and my sin is always before me.
Against you, you only, have I sinned
    and done what is evil in your sight,
so that you are proved right when you speak
    and justified when you judge.
Surely I have been a sinner from birth,
    sinful from the time my mother conceived me.
Surely you desire truth in the inward parts;
    you teach me wisdom in the inmost place.

Cleanse me with hyssop, and I will be clean;
    wash me, and I shall be whiter than snow.
Let me hear joy and gladness;
    let the bones you have crushed rejoice.
Hide your face from my sins
    and blot out all my iniquity.

Sitting in the church at Jim's funeral, Wendell felt like a hypocrite as he joined others in shedding tears for the sudden death of this young man. They were not close friends, but had grown up together in grade school, and saw each other almost every day. Jim was not very talented or good-looking and took more than his share of ribbing from the other kids, which evidently bothered him a lot. But Wendell was not particularly concerned – that was life, that's all, and he had much closer friends.

A couple of years ago, Jim had been in a car accident that resulted in his walking with a limp from then on. Wendell felt mildly sorry for him, but never said anything to Jim. He didn't know what to say, so he just said 'Hi' to him when they passed each other. Now Jim was dead, and Wendell joined the others in paying his respects to his memory. But to this day the nagging guilt feeling will not go away, though Wendell does not know why.

Have you 'felt guilty' today? This week I felt guilty because I fell behind with work preparation, I felt guilty when I missed a workout, I felt guilty when I did not restrain my tongue when I should have, I felt guilty when I failed to visit someone whom I had planned to visit, I felt guilty when I went to bed late, I felt guilty when I saw my shoes were dirty.

Should I have felt guilty?

Some psychoanalysts would say that our repressive parents conditioned us to feel guilty by telling us that we were bad. We can deal with these guilt feelings by talking about them to a therapist and then accepting that these feelings are just psychological and can be safely ignored or replaced with positive, ego-enhancing thoughts. This confession might involve reliving some unpleasant childhood experiences, but we would feel much better afterwards.

This system is similar to the Roman Catholic confessional. If you feel guilty, go to the priest and confess your sins, receive absolution, and go on your way happily without guilt until the next time you feel guilty and need absolution. Studies show that Roman Catholics have fewer problems with guilt-feelings than mainline Protestants precisely because of this mechanism.

David confessed to *God* his particular sins, his guilt, and his sinfulness since birth. David really took guilt seriously. 'My sin is always before me' (Psalm 51).

Should we take our 'guilt feelings' so seriously? When should we take them seriously, and how should we deal with them?

Florence van Horn became a nurse after her divorce in order to have a decent paying job to take care of her two children, and also to maintain a sense of self-worth. She worked long hours with throbbing joints and aching legs in the intensive care unit of a large hospital. Within a year, she had stolen her first pain-killing tablet from the narcotics cabinet. Gradually it became almost impossible to make it through the night without taking some drug. In time she realized she was an addict, guilty and fearful of being found out and fired. She changed jobs frequently, keeping one step ahead of discovery.

One night when she was on duty in a state psychiatric hospital, a young woman tried to commit suicide; as Florence bound up her slashed wrists, the woman bitterly told her she couldn't possibly understand what it was like to be abused by her parents. These words stung, because Florence had herself been abused by her father as a child. She went straight to the narcotics cabinet and took a pack of Demirol home with her. At night, while her sons were in the next room, she injected herself with the entire dosage – enough to kill her. Her guilty conscience told her that her sons would be better off without her. But 22 hours later she woke up.

Looking at the mess in the mirror that morning, she remembered one of the few pleasant childhood memories she possessed: a Sunday School classroom, where there was a picture of Jesus holding the lost lamb. Florence records, 'I knew I could not live any longer without him, and I cried out, "Jesus, please find me. Please help me. I am so lost." ' Next day she went to the Director of Nursing, confessed her addiction, and signed up for a drug treatment program, where she learned to face not only her addiction, but also her childhood abuse and the guilt she felt for all her life's failures. Nine years later, the recovery continues.

The Nature of Guilt
Guilt leads to a feeling of self-condemnation. It is an unhappy feeling. We feel bad, worthless, wrong, a failure, because of something we have done.

Sigmund Freud said that guilt is a conditioned response to which the solution is self-knowledge and self-acceptance. This means that we are not really responsible for anything. The failure of Freud's teachings to help anyone

in a lasting way has led modern psychologists and therapists to put forth other ideas.

Behavioral psychologists say that guilt feelings arise
from a failure to achieve our own standards of behavior.
Bad behavior (they may even use the word 'sin') occurs
when you hurt someone else. The solution is to learn to
live in a manner that harms no one. If we do this, we will
not feel guilty. But to such counselors sin is just a hori-
zontal matter; because they reject God, they do not understand that sin has a vertical dimension.

We must define guilt as David does: sin offends God.
The Bible teaches that we are all guilty beings, no matter
what popular but false teachers in the church say. 'There
is no one righteous, no, not one' (Romans 3:10). Guilt is
universal. All people are guilty in God's eyes because all
humans have rebelled against Him, gone their own way,
done what is evil in their hearts, and refused to be guided
by His will. God's law says, 'Love the Lord your God
with all your heart and with all your soul and with all your
mind and with all your strength' (Mark 12:30), but we
have all failed to do this. We are guilty and God is angry
with us.

We may not 'feel guilty' at times, but whatever we feel
inside, the truth is that we are guilty. We cannot evade this
truth.

The Symptoms of Guilt
The symptoms of guilt include a sense of inferiority, a
feeling of shame, a loss of the awareness of God's love
and acceptance, a sense of being condemned, a vague feel-

ing of depression, or even a feeling of violent self-hatred. The emotion varies with one's temperament and situation. In *The Trial* by Franz Kafka, the hero lives in a condition of never-ending unexplained feelings of guilt, to which there is no resolution or explanation.

The first human emotion after the Fall was a sense of guilt which led them to fear. When Adam and Eve heard the Lord approaching, they hid. Why? Because they knew they were guilty. Human guilt begins to develop in us at the age of two. After that, it is a constant companion lurking in the recesses of our minds.

True and False Guilt

Some 'guilt feelings' are legitimate, but some are not. Let us call them objectively-based and subjectively-based feelings.

We sometimes experience guilt for inadequate reasons. Perfectionists are very prone to this. Some Christians feel guilty because they are tempted – but Jesus Christ was tempted. Being tempted is not wrong, but giving in to temptation is. Others feel guilty because of mistakes – not deliberate wrongdoing, but everyday human error. This is not a sound basis for guilt, though we are guilty of vanity if we are proud of not making mistakes. We can have 'guilt-feelings' over all kinds of trivial acts and experiences, but this is often unnecessary.

Christians who have been converted after living very sinful lives may be burdened with guilt over their past. Although they know their sins have been forgiven, they are still full of regret that they did not come to know the

Lord sooner or abandon their sinful lifestyle sooner. This amounts to arguing with God's providence. It is wrong to 'feel guilty' over sins that have been forgiven; we are guilty only of doubting God's declaration of forgiveness! The Devil wants us to dwell on past sins and see ourselves as guilty when we should not because we are then poor witnesses to God's saving power.

True guilt occurs when we have violated God's law. If we did or said something that is clearly condemned in the Bible, we should 'feel' guilty because we are guilty. If we failed to do something commanded in the Bible, again we are guilty. We experience this awareness of guilt when the Holy Spirit is ministering to us through His Word, calling us to repentance. Since His purpose is to renew our fellowship with the Lord, these 'guilt-feelings' are purposeful and good.

This much is clear. But there is a third category in which false and true guilt are not so clear. The teenager who disobeys his parents to become mature and independent feels guilty for disobeying them, but when he obeys his parents, he feels guilty for not being mature and independent. The airman who drops the bomb may feel guilty for obeying the order to kill, while his colleague who disobeys the order to kill feels guilty for disobeying an order. The Corinthian Christians described in 1 Corinthians 8 felt guilty about eating meat and not eating meat. Paul said they should decide by an objective standard: the law of love to brothers.

An ordinary believer may have a sense of guilt because he or she does not love God enough, does not love people enough, does not work hard enough, resulting in no peace and a constant sense of guilt. Why is enough never enough?

In the case of the airman and teenager, the problem is that sometimes we are faced with two bad choices, either of which may result in us believing that we should have done better. Perhaps we should have, for sometimes we do make wrong choices. When that is the case, we need to confess and be forgiven and then go on.

The second example is of never being able to do enough to satisfy our conscience. How do you spend enough time with your children? How do you love your spouse enough? How do you work hard enough at your job? How do you love God enough?

The answer of course is that enough is never enough. We must accept that as a truth and realize that though our Father's standard is perfection, only Jesus can reach that standard and our Father knows that.

It is ignorance or pride that tells us we must achieve this wonderful record of goodness and love and obedience. The fact is that we are affected by sin, through and through, and everything we do is going to be less than perfect. This does not mean that we should not aim for perfection. We should aim for it in the knowledge that we cannot fully succeed; and we do not have to succeed in order to enjoy our Father's wonderful love, because Jesus Christ has done it for us.

D. Martyn Lloyd-Jones said, 'You say: "My trouble is that terrible sin which I have committed"; let me tell you in the name of God that that is not your trouble. Your trouble is unbelief. You do not believe the Word of God.' We often fail to believe the message of the gospel – that Christ was made sin for us so that all our guilt is removed forever and we now are completely righteous in God's sight. Post-conversion sins are real, but as soon as we confess these sins we have the assurance that all our sins are immediately forgiven because on the cross and by His resurrection Christ has taken away our guilt. Do we believe that God the Father punished Christ on the cross for our sins? Did Christ satisfy God's justice? We must believe this and reject the devil's accusations of guilt. Do not call unclean what God calls clean. If Christ cleansed us, we are clean forever!

We have this problem distinguishing between a valid and an invalid sense of guilt because our conscience – the God-given alarm for true guilt – has been affected by sin, so it is no longer completely reliable. In addition, our minds and consciences are constantly being bombarded with false and confusing messages from parents, friends, school, books, the media, government, and even some churches.

Managing our Guilt

Amanda knows her mother is dying. She has become a model daughter to her mother by taking care of her every need during this terminal illness, telling her every day that she loves her, and finding things in the past to thank her mother for. It was not always so. During most of their lives together in fact, there were times when she had been disrespectful towards her mother, had been impatient with her, ignored her. Not since she was a little girl had she told her mother that she loved her. She was too busy living her own life, doing her own thing.

When her mother's terminal illness was announced to

the family, Amanda was first shocked, naturally, but then became gradually overwhelmed with a sense of guilt — guilt for the hasty words, the long silences, the rude replies, the lack of real interest in the concerns of the one who had given her life. But Amanda repented before God and prayed for grace to love her mother in a way she did not feel. As she began to deny herself for her mother's sake, a bond developed between the two which caused many to marvel at the Christlike love of daughter for mother.

> The LORD is compassionate and gracious,
>> slow to anger, abounding in love.
> He will not always accuse,
>> nor will he harbor his anger for ever;
> he does not treat us as our sins deserve
>> or repay us according to our iniquities.
> For as high as the heavens are above the earth,
>> so great is his love for those who fear him;
> As far as the east is from the west,
>> so far has he removed our transgressions from us
>>> **(Psalm 103:8-12).**

David's psalm of repentance, Psalm 51, offers us the outline of a solution to the problem of guilt, as does Psalm 103 and many others.

1. We should identify God. Is He our enemy? No, the message of the gospel is that He is now, through Christ's work,

our friend and our lover. He is not against us, He is for us (Psalm 103:8). This is the God we know. This is the God described in the parable of the Prodigal Son (Luke 15). His arms are open to us.

2. We must recognize that the Bible is the standard by which we know if our sense of guilt is valid or invalid. 'I would not have known what sin was except through the law' (Romans 7:7). We should hold up the cause of our guilt to the mirror of Scripture to determine if what we are concerned about is a real sin.

3. If it is a real sin, we must not deny it, suppress it, or shift the blame for it to someone else. 'He who conceals his sins does not prosper, but whoever confesses and renounces them finds mercy' (Proverbs 28:13). We should acknowledge sin quickly and experience that sense of relief that David expressed in Psalm 51 after he stopped repressing and denying his sin. How refreshing it is to get it out into the open before God, though at the time it is humbling, too. Many people have tried to bury their sins in their past, like a dog with an old bone. We should instead lay them at the foot of the cross and get rid of them forever.

4. We should define the gospel again to ourselves. 'There is now no condemnation for those who are in Christ Jesus' (Romans 8:1). To get rid of guilt, all we have to do is

confess it and believe that Jesus Christ died to take it away. Even David saw this from afar (Psalm 103:11-12).

In the New Testament, freedom from the guilt of sin is made wonderfully clear: 'If we walk in the light, as He is in the light, we have fellowship with one another, and the blood of Jesus, His Son, purifies us from every sin. If we claim to be without sin, we deceive ourselves and the truth is not in us. If we confess our sins, He is faithful and just and will forgive us our sins and purify us from all unrighteousness' (1 John 1:7-9).

These are the promises of the Father. The Father always welcomes the prodigal back. But when we come back, we return as His children, clothed in Christ's righteousness. We can know that whatever we have done, the Father accepts us and loves us, so we should never let guilt come between us and God our Father.

The Word of God affirms clearly that God has dropped the charges against us once and for all on the grounds that His justice has been satisfied and our sins fully punished in Christ Jesus, our substitute.

5. We should respond to the gospel again. If we believe the gospel, we must ask for forgiveness and believe we are forgiven. There is no need to go on and on asking for forgiveness. Our Father does not need to be persuaded; Jesus Christ is our advocate, and His prayers for our forgiveness are always heard. We are forgiven at once when we confess. So we may believe and get up and go on, without guilt.

Then we may enjoy the peace of God that comes from

justification by faith only. Praise God that He has declared you not guilty again! How good it is that we do not have to compensate for our bad deeds with good deeds, as popular Roman Catholic theology suggests. All we have to do is believe and receive the free and full forgiveness of God.

Paul said, 'I care very little if I am judged by you or by any human courts; indeed I do not even judge myself. My conscience is clear, but that does not make me innocent. It is the Lord who judges me' (1 Corinthians 4:3-4). The Lord has already judged and acquitted believers and declared them to be fully righteous in His sight. We need to say the same as the apostle: I will not feel guilty or judge myself because my Father has already judged me in Christ and declared me innocent and righteous in His sight.

Do not let the devil rob you of peace with true or false guilt. 'Therefore, since we have been justified through faith, we have peace with God through our Lord Jesus Christ' (Romans 5:1). Take that peace and enjoy it!

5

Hatred

Who, Me, Hate?

Psalm 139:17-24

How precious to me are your thoughts, O God!
　　How vast is the sum of them!
Were I to count them
　　they would outnumber the grains of sand.
When I am awake
　　I am still with you.

If only you would slay the wicked, O God!
Away from me, you bloodthirsty men!
They speak of you with evil intent;
　　your adversaries misuse your name.
Do I not hate those who hate you, O LORD,
　　and abhor those who rise up against you?
I have nothing but hatred for them;
　　I count them my enemies.

Search me, O God, and know my heart;
　　test me and know my anxious thoughts.
See if there is any offensive way in me,
　　and lead me in the way everlasting.

I have a clear memory of the reaction to a sermon I preached twenty years ago on Matthew 18:15-18, about the need for Christians to confront one another lovingly over offenses. After the usual polite comments by various people on the way out of worship, I turned to meet two elderly ladies who were weeping copiously; they proceeded to thank me profusely for my wonderful sermon; it had made a profound impact on them they said, and they felt so happy now. They continued in this vein for some time, thanking me and praising my wonderful sermon.

Well, I knew my sermon wasn't that wonderful, so I inquired as to what exactly had struck them about the message. 'Well, you see,' one of them explained, 'we haven't been speaking to one another; and now that we understand what the Lord said in Matthew, we have apologized to one another, and we feel so much better.' Gratified, but still a little puzzled, I asked, 'How long had you not been speaking to one another?' Their answer chilled my blood: 'Forty years.'

One had made a critical remark about the child of the other forty years ago and for forty years they had sat on opposite sides of the church in worship, ignoring one another. If you had asked them in all those years if they hated anyone, they would have denied it at once; but they did hate – until they understood the Biblical way of dealing with offenses.

Many Christians will deny that they are ever guilty of hatred. They see it as a contradiction of their Christian testimony and something only really bad people indulge in. Sadly, this is not true.

Hatred is the converse of love. Indifference is the absence of emotion. Both love and hatred are very powerful feelings, and strangely, one can turn to its opposite quite easily. When love turns to hatred, it is a very destructive influence – both to the hater and to the hated one.

Hatred is a complicated theme. The Lord hates – the one who is the God of love hates. God commands us to hate and forbids us to hate. We should reflect God's image as creatures capable of feeling hatred.

Attitude of Hatred

Hatred is the opposite of love. It can exist in many different degrees, from a mild rejection of someone or something to a violent desire to destroy.

The Bible says that God hates. When the Lord said in Romans 9:13, 'Jacob I loved and Esau I hated,' he was saying that Jacob was His preferred choice, and He did not choose Esau – He passed him by.

In a similar sense, Jesus said, 'If anyone comes to me and does not hate his father and mother, his wife and children, his brothers and sisters – yes, even his own life – he cannot be my disciple' (Luke 14:26). We are to make Jesus our first loyalty and love and put the desires and claims of our families firmly in second place as Jesus Christ did Himself with His own earthly parents. Jesus Christ also said, 'The man who loves his life will lose it, while the man who hates his life in this world will keep it for eternal life' (John 12:25). In other words, the believer in Jesus Christ is to prefer Christ's will to his own. To hate your own life means to be willing to give it up for something that is more important.

Emotion is not necessarily involved in this type of hatred, which is actually a settled attitude of mind. In this sense God hates wickedness and sin.

'You hate all who do wrong. You destroy those who tell lies; bloodthirsty and deceitful men the LORD abhors' (Psalm 5:5,6).

'The LORD examines the righteous, but the wicked and those who love violence His soul hates' (Psalm 11:5).

And the Lord calls us to hate all that opposes God.

Jesus Christ said, 'No one can serve two masters. Either he will hate the one and love the other, or he will be devoted to the one and despise the other' (Matthew 6:24). The child of God cannot be indifferent to sin and injustice; we must either abhor and reject it or be controlled by it.

David said, 'I abhor the assembly of evildoers and refuse to sit with the wicked' (Psalm 26:5), and 'I hate those who cling to worthless idols' (Psalm 31:6). This was also the thought and attitude he expressed in Psalm 139:21,22. Since he spoke as the anointed king of Israel, appointed to defend and protect God's people and lead them in obedience, it was appropriate for him to abhor the enemies of God and His people.

But under the new covenant there is a change; the church is now in the world, not separated from it as Israel was. We are in it, though not part of it. Now Jesus Christ warns us that the world will hate us, but we are not to hate worldly people. We are to love them, as Christ did us.

The rabbis of Jesus' day told their followers to hate the Epicureans and other pagans, and the members of the Qumran Sect were told to hate the Sons of Darkness, referring to everyone outside the sect. But Jesus Christ told His followers to love their enemies and do good to those who hated them (Matthew 5:43).

Now in all these cases, we are talking about an attitude of heart and mind. It is not an attitude that our contemporary culture finds easy to comprehend, because it is contrary to the popular teaching of tolerance as the only absolute virtue. Our culture asserts that we are to tolerate any opinion or activity, however perverse it may be in the eyes of the Lord. But according to the Scriptures, that is not to be the attitude of the child of God. We are called on the one hand not to tolerate any from of evil, and on the other hand to love those who are wicked and tell them of the gospel and do them good.

The natural man hates God and loves himself (Romans 1). So he also hates anyone who stands in his way. That is the way of the world.

In contrast the child of God loves his Father in heaven and learns to hate self-love and evil and to love others despite their evil acts. This is the mark of Christians.

However the emotion of hatred is different from the settled attitude of hatred of evil.

Feeling of Hatred

Because hatred is part of our nature, it can flare up in different situations. Remember that hatred is the converse of love. Just as we cannot explain how the feeling of love suddenly develops, so we cannot always explain the feeling of hatred.

Just as love tries to build up, protect, and care for someone, hatred tries to harm and destroy people. Hatred is often related to fear of what someone might do to us. We may hate our boss because he might fire us. We may hate the lady next door because we fear her gossip about us.

Consider Lela who was born with a dreadful skin disease that warped her life as she was growing up and she allowed it to warp her attitude to life as well. Some doctors called it eczema. Others identified it as atopic dermatitis. She went to school covered in smelly, sticky yellow ointment; sometimes her eyes were swollen nearly shut; sometimes her clothing stuck to her body, despite the coatings of greasy remedies. Her adolescence was miserable, despite being way ahead of other children academically. She confesses 'Along with my physical problems, I developed a bitter, cynical spirit. I hated my middle-aged, fundamentalist Christian parents. I resented my mocking schoolmates. Most of all, I despised myself.'

This life of hatred began to lift when she went forward at a Billy Graham crusade when she was 16. But it was four years later before she became convinced that God wanted to heal her and indeed could heal her. Her cynicism and hatred fought with new hope, until one day at the age of 20, clear patches of skin began to appear on her body. Despite the fact she was taking no medication now, the clear skin spread, until in a few days her body was completely clear and smooth. Believe it or not, she has gone on to do runway modelling ! But more importantly, her inner attitude of hatred of life and of herself has died.

Hatred hurts the hater as much as the hated. Joseph's brothers hated him because of fear and jealousy (Genesis 37:2-4). David's son, Ammon, hated his sister because of guilt, self-disgust, and the fear of consequences (2 Samuel 13). Absalom hated Ammon because his love for Tamar was bruised and hurt (2 Samuel 13:22). There is an interesting example of the interrelationship of love and hate in 2 Samuel 19:1-7. Because of his feelings, David treated those he loved badly. He was a confused man at that time, but it is true of all of us that love can quickly turn to hatred if our feelings of love are damaged.

1 John 3:15 gives us a severe warning: 'Anyone who hates his brother is a murderer, and you know that no murderer has eternal life in him.' Hatred is spiritual murder, and we have all been guilty of this feeling at some time.

Symptoms of Hatred
Proverbs 10:12 says that hatred stirs up strife. Conflict in personal relationships is one symptom of this feeling.

When we fail to achieve our dreams or fall short of our own standards of behavior, we may experience a feeling of self-hatred. This leads to depression, self-pity, and sometimes even suicide. This appears to be fairly common in Japan. Sexual offenders, especially homosexuals, are often filled with self-hatred because they know deep down inside that they are not the way they should be and want to be.

In 2 Samuel 19, Joab confronted David with the symptom of his hatred − he was not caring for his own men. Love means caring; hatred means rejection. At that moment, David in effect was hating those he loved.

If the feeling is violent and strong, hatred may make our limbs shake and tremble, and it may churn our stomach as fear does. Hatred may warp our view of others and of all of life, so that we see nothing good anywhere, unless we deal with it quickly.

Occasions for Hatred

There are a myriad sources for the feelings of hatred that arise in our hearts. Joseph's brothers were envious and fearful of Joseph, which led to bitterness, and bitterness led to hatred. Cain first was disappointed, then angry, then he hated his brother, Abel. Ammon transferred his guilt to his sister and grew to hate her, and Absalom hated Ammon because he had loved his betrayed sister so dearly.

Charles and Jeri Boley lost their son Brian at the age of 20 in a drunk driving accident. The drunk driver, Ruben Gonzalez, was convicted of manslaughter; but as several appeals delayed sentencing, Jeri Boley grew impatient for 'justice'. Actually what she wanted was revenge; she hated this man who had taken her son. Charles said to her on the night before the sentencing: 'Jeri, we've got to leave justice to God.' But Jeri wanted a justice she could see and feel. She was not interested in extending compassion to this killer who was arguing for time to be with his own son Brian, who was dying.

She felt nothing next day when Gonzalez was sentenced to an immediate term in prison. She told him she forgave him. But that night she was as tortured and restless as ever. Gonzalez had said he was sorry, but Jeri's attitude had in reality changed little, despite her words of forgiveness.

The following day Jeri and Charles spoke to the judge
and asked that Gonzalez be allowed to remain free to care
for his dying son before serving his sentence.

In making this ruling in the courtroom, the judge stated:
'From what I have learned of Brian Boley in the course of
this trial, I think he would be pleased with all of us.' Afterwards, Jeri records that 'As the guards came up and
released Ruben Gonzalez, I could feel the chains fall away
from around my heart ... I was finally able to say to my
own son, "Good-bye, Brian." ' Freedom from hate often
comes from doing good to the object of our hate.

When others cause us pain or suffering, we may feel
resentment and then hatred toward them. But we can also
feel hatred for people who subconsciously remind us of
someone else who hurt us long ago. A girl may feel hatred
for all men when she grows up because she was sexually
abused as a child. A man may hate all Vietnamese people
because he lost so many friends in Vietnam. Fifty years
after World War II, some British and Dutch people still
abhor all Germans because of painful memories.

We should not, however, blame other people. Other people and events do not cause us to hate. They stimulate or
tempt us to hate, but the real reason we hate is that it is
part of our nature. Our Savior said, 'Out of the heart come
evil thoughts, murder, adultery, sexual immorality, theft,
false testimony, slanders' (Matthew 15:19). The human
heart is a Pandora's box of ugly thoughts and emotions
we would like to deny and disown. Karl Menniger, a psy-
chologist who rejects Freud's blame-shifting theories, said,
'The child does not learn to hate; he comes into the world
equipped with it, for better or for worse, and then he learns

to use it, wisely or unwisely, according to his experiences.'

As Christians, we must learn to recognize and use hatred wisely – not according to our experiences, but according to God's Word.

Managing Hatred

The Bible says, 'Do not hate your brother in your heart. Rebuke your neighbor frankly so that you will not share in his guilt' (Leviticus 19:17), and 'Get rid of all bitterness, rage and anger, brawling and slander, along with every form of malice. Be kind and compassionate to one another, forgiving each other, just as in Christ God forgave you' (Ephesians 4:31).

What are we to do about feelings of hatred?

1. Acknowledge and confess this aspect of our sinful nature. 'At one time we too were foolish, disobedient, deceived and enslaved by all kinds of passions and pleasures. We lived in malice and envy, being hated and hating one another' (Titus 3:3). The old lifestyle included hatred, but it must not be allowed to continue. We must confess that we are guilty of hatred.

2. Use hatred positively by hating evil as God does – first in ourselves, and then in the world. 'You have this in your favor,' Jesus said to the Ephesian church, 'you hate the practices of the Nicolaitans, which I also hate' (Revela-

tion 2:6). Hate heresy and wickedness. Abhor it, reject it, shun it.

3. Turn hatred of people into love, as Jesus Christ commanded us. We are to love those who hate us by caring for them, doing good for them, and building them up. 'You have heard that it was said, "Love your neighbor and hate your enemy." But I tell you: Love your enemies and pray for those who persecute you, that you may be sons of your Father in heaven. He causes His sun to rise on the evil and the good, and sends rain on the righteous and the unrighteous' (Matthew 5:43,44).

Although it may be very hard, if we show love even when we do not feel it, the negative feelings will gradually diminish and be replaced by positive feelings. We can only do this as we meditate on God's undeserved love for us and ask Him to send the Spirit of His Son to fill our hearts with love for God and love for our neighbor.

Though it goes against our nature, it is the whole duty of the believer to love God with all our heart, and mind, and soul, and strength, and to love our neighbor as ourself.

Overcome hate with love. That is the power of the gospel, and that is our calling as we imitate the attitude, feelings and actions of our heavenly Father.

6

Envy / Jealousy

The Green-Eyed Serpent

Psalm 37:1-9

Do not fret because of evil men
  or be envious of those who do wrong;
for like the grass they will soon wither,
  like green plants they will soon die away.

Trust in the LORD and do good;
  dwell in the land and enjoy safe pasture.
Delight yourself in the LORD
  and he will give you the desires of your heart.
Commit your way to the LORD;
  trust in him and he will do this;
He will make your righteousness shine like the dawn,
  the justice of your cause like the noonday sun.

Be still before the LORD and wait patiently for him;
  do not fret when men succeed in their ways,
  when they carry out their wicked schemes.

Refrain from anger, turn from wrath;
  do not fret—it leads only to evil.
For evil men will be cut off,
  but those who hope in the LORD will inherit the land.

Psalm 73:1-17

Surely God is good to Israel,
  to those who are pure in heart.

But as for me, my feet had almost slipped;
  I had nearly lost my foothold.
For I envied the arrogant
  when I saw the prosperity of the wicked.

They have no struggles;
  their bodies are healthy and strong.
They are free from the burdens common to man;
  they are not plagued by human ills ....

Surely in vain have I kept my heart pure;
  in vain have I washed my hands in innocence
All day long I have been plagued;
  I have been punished every morning.

If I had said, 'I will speak thus,'
  I would have betrayed your children.
When I tried to understand all this,
  it was oppressive to me
till I entered the sanctuary of God;
  then I understood their final destiny.

The New York Times Magazine of April 23, 1995 contained a study of recent lottery millionaires – people who had won between $1 and $31.5 million.[3] The lives of most of them had, apparently, been destroyed by their sudden wealth, mainly due to the reactions of their friends and families and strangers and their responses to these reactions. Many of them did not understand that $1 million is doled out at $50,000 a year over 20 or 25 years – before taxes. But it is the attitude of friends and relatives that is most shocking; many winners said they were happier before they won!

Debbie from Colorado records: 'One sister didn't speak to us for a year because we didn't pick up a breakfast check; another expected us to repay her school loans. A close friend borrowed money and we didn't hear from him again for three years – when he called to borrow some more.' Teresa was 25 when she won $1.3 million; there was a party to celebrate. 'Of all the people who came, not one speaks to me now,' she recalls.

Bernice took a day off work to claim her million; when she went back to work, she was told her job had been given away. She and her family moved to South Dakota; she and her husband divorced. Now she tells no one her secret. When Cindy won $2.5 million ten years ago the first person to call was her best friend; not to congratulate her but to protest angrily, 'What right did you have to win ?' Her mother did not speak to her for six years because she thought the money should be shared with her sister who had scratched the numbers on the lottery card.

---

3. *The New York Times Sunday Magazine*, April 23, 1995.

Bud Post won a $16.2 million Pennsylvania jackpot in 1988 and was dead broke five years later. Worse, his brother was in jail charged with hiring a hit man to murder Bud and his sixth wife for the lottery money. Mary Ellen Snipes spent three and a half years in court fighting her ex-husband's claim for half the fortune of $31.5 million.

Most bizarre, perhaps, is the story of Daisy Fernandez, who won $2.8 million, and then was sued by the teenage son of her friend, whom she had asked to pray for her. Christopher had prayed to his favorite saint; and when his prayer was answered, he claimed half the winnings. He lost. But so also did all the others who put envy and jealousy before friendship and contentment.

Psalm 37 and Psalm 73 are remarkably honest about an ugly emotion that few people want to admit: envy or jealousy. The words of these songs were written after the writer repented, but everyone at some time feels the surge of the green-eyed monster.

Shakespeare coined that term in the mouth of Iago: 'O beware, my lord, of jealousy; it is the green-eyed monster.' An apocryphal book, the *Wisdom of Solomon*, says, 'Through envy of the devil came death into the world.' Many theologians agree that envy of God's glory was probably the sin that first arose in Satan's heart.

A story is told of a mysterious traveler who met two envious men on a road. He told them that whichever made a wish first would get exactly what he wished for, but his companion would get twice as much. Neither of these two jealous characters would make the first wish for fear the other would get double! After arguing and shouting, one finally grabbed the other by the throat and said he would kill him if he did not make his wish first. The second man relented, wishing that he would be blind in one eye. So he was, and the other man became blind in both!

This grimly amusing story shows the corrosive power of envy. A proverb says, 'Envy shoots others and wounds itself' (Ecclesiasticus). And another says, 'Envy and wrath shorten the life.' The Grinch, a character in Dr. Seuss' books, cannot stand the sight of anyone having a good time; he gets so jealous that he bites himself.

Nature of Envy and Jealousy

Distinguishing between envy and jealousy is difficult. Envy is directed toward the possessions of other, and jealousy is concerned with the character of others. Two stories may illustrate the difference.

A 69-carat diamond was displayed in Cartier's store on Fifth Avenue in New York City, and a record price was paid for it. While it was on display, crowds of people filed by to view the famous gem. A security guard overheard some of the comments: 'I see a slight flaw in it'; 'it's too large'; 'it's vulgar really, but I had to see it'; 'it's not that beautiful, but I wouldn't mind having it.' The security guard said later, 'I've heard more sour grapes in the last two days than in the whole of my life!'

We begrudge others having what we do not have. That is envy. Envy is a feeling that life is not fair because someone else has a new dress, a new car, a new baby, a longer vacation. We become resentful because we feel deprived that someone else has what we don't have.

The world is full of people who have more and better of everything that we have – at least if we ignore the Third World countries, China, and Eastern Europe – almost 90 per cent of humanity! Envy shuts our eyes to those with less than we have and focuses only on those who have more than we have.

The other story is of an old saint who lived in the desert as a hermit. Demons and people tempted him in vain. concerning hunger, thirst, possessions, doubt, and fear. He resisted all temptations to sin. But then the Devil came to him and said, 'Congratulations! Your brother has just been made bishop of Alexandria!' At once a frown appeared on the hermit's face.

That's jealousy! Another person is seen to be more powerful, more successful, more attractive, or more privileged than I. Jealousy is longer-lasting than envy. The Song of Solomon reminds us that jealousy is the handmaid of love: 'Love is strong as death; jealousy is cruel as the grave' (8:6). When Leonardo grew old he became jealous of Michelangelo. Salieri was jealous of Mozart. An ironic proverb says, 'No man is a complete failure until he begins disliking men who succeed.'

Jealousy is even found among churches and preachers. The famous and gifted F. B. Meyer confessed to being jealous of the success of Dr. Campbell Morgan when they were both preaching in London. Any time our Lord blesses a church, or denomination, or ministry with growth and achievement, other churches point out its faults.

The apostle Paul had a zeal for God and for His law

before his conversion to Jesus Christ (Galatians 1:14), so much so that he persecuted the church of Christ (Acts 22:3,4). The Greek word for zeal is the same as jealousy. Saul the persecutor was also driven by jealousy of the success of the growing church and the godly lives of the people he thought were heretics. His jealous zeal led him to destroy and kill.

Zeal for God's glory is good. When it leads you to attack other people in God's name, it is not zeal, but jealousy.

James 4:5 tells us that God is jealous, or zealous, for you. God as Creator, Savior, and Lover has the sovereign right to be jealous for your affections. This is the good use of the word jealousy in the Bible. As the Christian is the rightful object of God's jealous love, so the Christian should be jealous for the Name and glory of the Lord.

Occasions for Envy and Jealousy

When they were teenagers, Ricky and Cindy carved their love for one another inside a heart on an old bridge in Trenton, Florida. Twenty years later, they remember how their relationship almost aborted before they married. Shortly after they started dating, they were working with some other people in her father's field, when Ricky accused Cindy of flirting with one of the workers. Later he apologized. But whenever Cindy spoke to another man, Ricky would fly into a violent rage. Whenever another man even said hello, Ricky would get mad and attack his girlfriend.

One day Cindy's father took Ricky aside and suggested

that Ricky read I Corinthians 13, especially verse 4, and Ricky did. But soon after, when they were eating in a pizzeria, some football players entered and one of them gave Cindy a big smile and a hello. At once they had to leave and Ricky ranted and raved all the way home because, he said, he loved her so. But before parting that night Cindy told him: 'Ricky, I can't take it any more. I can't marry you if you're going to be like this.'

On the long drive home, Ricky prayed to God for grace to help his insane jealousy; he remembered I Corinthians 13:4 – 'Love is not jealous' – and gradually he came to understand what that means. True love is not controlling. True love trusts. So Ricky prayed: 'Dear God, take away my jealous heart. Help me to learn to trust you and those who love me. I've tried to do it myself and I can't. Amen.' God answered that prayer, and Cindy and Ricky were able to get married, and twenty years later, their love remains.

The primary cause of envy and jealousy is fairly simple – self-love. When a new baby is born, the older sibling becomes jealous. Why? Because until then, the only child was the center of attention. Now the loving parents are suddenly spending more time with the new baby, which the older child does not like at all. Sometimes a pet dog or cat will show the same symptoms of jealousy when no longer feeling it is the center of attention. The idol of self-love is a jealous master.

Jessica had a wonderful junior year in high school. She was one of eight girls on the basketball team that spent hours working together to perfect their ball skills, and their harmonious relationship payed off in terms of team victories. These girls also stayed together outside of practice –

they hung out with each other and went shopping together. They were a real team, and they had a great time.

Then senior year came along, and the previous team captain was gone and so they had to choose a new team leader. When the choice was announced, it was as if a poison-gas bomb had been set off. Every one of these previously inseparable friends was jealous of the one selected, and bickering and catty remarks became the order of the day, and soon friendship was almost non-existent.

Jessica's senior year was a miserable experience. She looked forward to going to physical therapy school, together with her one remaining friend, Stephanie. When Jessica's College letter of rejection arrived, she was deeply disappointed. Then when she found out that her friend Stephanie, whose grades were the same as hers, had been accepted, she flew into a jealous rage, and for weeks could not speak to Stephanie. Jessica became bitter in spirit and hostile to her friends. She eventually admitted the truth to herself: she was a jealous person, and needed to do something about this fact before it destroyed her life.

Self-love wants attention, it wants to be popular. Rejoicing in the success or fame of others is often hard for us to do. Why was Julius Caesar killed? Mark Anthony stated, 'This was the noblest Roman of them all. All the conspirators save only he did what they did in envy of great Caesar.' Shakespeare, in *As You Like It*, describes the fourth stage of a man's life: 'Jealous in honor, sudden and quick to quarrel, seeking the bubble reputation.'

Shakespeare points to two causes of envy and jealousy: resentment of another's power and resentment of another's fame.

Hollywood is a cesspool of jealousy and envy. With success measured in terms of fame, performers are jealous of other stars' popularity and money. Some business corporations are not much different. Even scientists bitterly attack another who makes a breakthrough in research. Athletes, preachers, doctors and lawyers often see life as a competition with other people and are filled with jealousy when others succeed. They feel diminished, put down, and rejected because another is blessed. Even David envied the wicked because of their prosperous lifestyle (Psalm 73).

Paul says the cause of envy and jealousy is the flesh, the fallen nature, which is contrasted with the spirit (Galatians 5:22-26). Peter says the same (1 Peter 2:1,2).

Symptoms of Envy and Jealousy

The crucifixion narratives present a striking example of jealousy. Mark tells us that envy and jealousy led to the crucifixion of our Lord (Mark 15:9-11). Those who crucified Jesus were so filled with jealousy that they desired to hurt and destroy the object of their jealousy. The story of Cain and Abel demonstrates the same feelings. Jealousy leads to anger and depression, which leads to hatred or even murder. In some cases the resentment and bitterness that flow from envy and jealousy are invisible to others, festering slowly and cancerously within, robbing the individual of joy and peace, with caustic and cynical remarks the only symptoms, and the root cause hard to identify. Sometimes the only symptom is the frown of envy.

Many young lovers have allowed jealousy to warp and

control their entire lives for years, blinding them to the possibilities of peace and happiness around them.

If we do not deal with this ugly emotion, it will grow like those vines that climb up a tall tree and slowly smother it, preventing the life-giving rays of the sun from touching the tree until it dies, choked to death by this parasite. The Christian solution is laid out for us in Psalms 37 and 73, at the beginning of this chapter.

Managing Envy and Jealousy
The solution for envy and jealousy is similar to that for the other negative emotions.

1. Acknowledge that you are jealous. Denying or repressing this emotion is pointless. You must take this ugly feeling before the Lord and acknowledge it. David described doing this: 'I envied the arrogant when I saw the prosperity of the wicked .... When I tried to understand all this, it was oppressive to me till I entered the sanctuary of God' (Psalm 73:3, 16, 17a). David acknowledged his wrong feelings and thoughts, first to himself, then to the Lord. So did Simon the Sorcerer (Acts 8), avoiding divine judgment on himself.

2. Confess your sin and repent. This is what the psalmist did: 'When my heart was grieved and my spirit embittered, I was senseless and ignorant; ... my flesh and my heart may fail, but God is the strength of my heart and my

portion forever' (Psalm 73:21,22,26). Consider the gospel and how you are to live as one committed to Christ.

3. View life and people from God's perspective. See individuals and their circumstances as created by God according to His will and for His purposes, and not yours to control. Then pray for those you envy and seek to help them. Although it is hard, when we substitute godly attitudes and behavior for envy and jealousy, sinful feelings toward others will wither and die. No two human beings are exactly equal. God has made us all different with different gifts and possessions and roles, each designed to glorify Him in different ways. That should not be a cause of resentment, but of wonder and admiration.

In addition, learn to see individuals and their circumstances in the light of eternity, as our Lord does. This is the great lesson David learned: 'Do not fret because of evil men or be envious of those who do wrong; for like the grass they will soon wither, like green plants they will soon die away. Trust in the LORD and do good ... delight yourself in the LORD and He will give you the desires of your heart' (Psalm 37:1-4). 'When I tried to understand all this, it was oppressive to me till I entered the sanctuary of God; then I understood their destiny' (Psalm 73:16,17).

If all the blessings of the wicked are temporary and yours are eternal, what is there to envy? It's a puff of smoke, an illusion. None of it matters. And if it is other believers that you are jealous of, remember, 'To whom much is given much is required.' Do you really want to be more accountable to the Lord than you already are?

4. Live by faith, not by appearances. After looking around at the objects of his envy, David concluded Psalm 37 by saying, 'Delight yourself in the LORD and He will give you the desires of your heart' (desires that are godly and not selfish or silly!). Believe that God is your Father, and He has not forsaken you and never will. Believe that He is trustworthy and delight in Him. In Christ you have everything you need for this life and eternity. Your desires may not be your real needs. Trust Him.

David expressed his confidence in a loving Father: 'Yet I am always with you; you hold me by my right hand. You guide me with your counsel, and afterwards you will take me into glory. Whom have I in heaven but you? And earth has nothing I desire besides you. My flesh and my heart may fail, but God is the strength of my heart and my portion forever' (Psalm 73:23-26). If the Lord helps, guides, counsels, provides, and protects you, surely other things do not really matter. It is good to be near God. There is nothing better or richer than that.

5. Develop a contented spirit. When David said to wait on the Lord, he meant to be content with what the Lord gives. 'Be still before the LORD and wait patiently for Him; do not fret .... Better the little that the righteous have than the wealth of many wicked ... the LORD loves the just and will not forsake His faithful ones' (Psalm 37:7, 16, 28a).

Paul said, 'Godliness with contentment is great gain' (1 Timothy 6:6). While in jail in Philippi, Paul observed, 'It is true that some preach Christ out of envy and rivalry, but others out of good will ... but what does it matter? The important thing is that in every way ... Christ is preached. And because of this I rejoice' (Philippians 1:15,18). He was content while others were filled with envy. But he told us, 'I have learned to be content whatever the circumstances' (Philippians 4:11).

The author of Hebrews says the same: 'Be content with what you have.' How? By trusting in Jesus Christ and His providence and believing that everything you don't have and everything you are not is working together for your eternal profit by the grace of God. Do you believe that? Then preach it to yourself when the green-eyed monster bites your heart.

7

Grief

Weeping with Hope

Psalm 13:1-3

How long, O LORD? Will you forget me forever?
   How long will you hide your face from me?
How long must I wrestle with my thoughts
   and every day have sorrow in my heart?
Look on me and answer, O LORD my God.
   Give light to my eyes, or I will sleep in death ....

Leo was a seven-year-old boy whose best friend was a cat called Little Yellow; he carried her around the house and she slept, purring, in his lap. One afternoon, Little Yellow was struck by a car in the street, and Leo found Little Yellow's still, limp body on the pavement. Devastated, Leo ran to his mother's arms and cried and cried. His mother tried to calm him, but he would not be consoled. His body shook and his tears soaked his mothers apron.

He was startled to hear his mothers voice, after a while, ask, 'Leo, what are you holding on to?' Wonderingly, he listened to his mother explain that we can't hold on to things or people in this world; everything is transient, nothing and nobody lasts forever; toys get broken, grandpa must die, all must go sometime. We cannot hold on – so we must let go. This wisdom has helped Leo deal with many crises over the years, and it can help us too; it is, in fact, the message of Ecclesiastes.

You may doubt that it is appropriate to include the emotion of grief in a study of negative emotions. After all, the Bible portrays grief at the death of a loved one as something entirely natural and appropriate, does it not? Moreover, we are encouraged by our Lord Jesus to grieve over sin.

Nevertheless, grief has driven many people to illness and death. Like all human emotions, grief can be experienced in both positive and negative, helpful and harmful ways.

At this moment you may be perfectly happy, and thinking about grief may seem unnecessary and morbid. But it is wise to be prepared for the future, rather than to have it sneak up on us when we least expect it! It is best to consider the nature, causes, and solutions to grief before we find ourselves mourning. If we do not know how to grieve in a biblical fashion, our grief will be much more painful.

Most of us live in a culture where people do not know how to grieve because we have been told that everyone has a right to be happy all the time. That is an unrealistic and misguided notion. In a world of suffering, pain, injustice, illness, and death, no sane person will feel perpetually happy.

If anyone in all of human history could have been continuously and gloriously happy, it was our Lord Jesus. But Isaiah described the Messiah as a man of sorrows and acquainted with grief (Isaiah 53) – and so he was. At the grave of Lazarus, Jesus did not say, 'Don't worry – be happy,' rather, He wept. The Son of God cried openly and sincerely (John 11:35).

Ecclesiastes reminds us that there is 'a time to laugh, and a time to weep'. Beware of the call of a pagan culture to run away from grief and to deny the need to mourn. Such a reaction to suffering makes the pain of grief worse. The gospel of God is for real hurting, crying people.

Nature of Grief

Psalm 13 conveys a strong sense of grief: 'How long, O LORD? Will you forget me forever? How long will you hide your face from me? How long must I wrestle with my thoughts and every day have sorrow in my heart? How long will my enemy triumph over me? Look on me and answer, O LORD, my God. Give light to my eyes, or I will sleep in death.'

One writer on this subject said, 'Grief is a life-shaking sorrow over loss.' Another stated, 'Grief is a complex,

painful process of dealing with and adjusting to loss.' Grief
is complex because it is very closely connected to other
emotions that erupt and subside within the grieving person – anger, bitterness, fear, guilt, self-pity. This complex set of emotions is usually triggered by some kind of
personal loss. Even animals can grieve over the sudden
loss of a master or mistress, and it is a pathetic sight.

The depth of the feeling of grief varies according to the
nature of the loss and the temperament of the suffering
individual. Its pain depends on the closeness of the relationship that has been broken. Some losses can be overcome quickly, but others can devastate a person's life for
years. The average length of time for serious grief is two
to four months.

Causes of Grief

David's grief over the imminent death of his baby son is
one of the clearest descriptions of grief in the Bible.

'The LORD struck the child that Uriah's wife had born
to David, and he became ill. David pleaded with God
for the child. He fasted and went into his house and
spent the nights lying on the ground. The elders of his
household stood beside him to get him up from the
ground, but he refused, and he would not eat any food
with them' (2 Samuel 12:15-17).

We usually associate grief with the loss of a person
very close to us. But people also experience other kinds of
losses – a job, a home, a pet, a marriage, a business, a

reputation, a favorite activity. However, the most painful and fearful losses are those of a spouse, a child, a parent, a sibling, or a close friend. Such a great loss shatters the illusion that we are in control of our lives; and we feel abandoned, helpless, betrayed, and vulnerable.

One of the worst things we can say to a bereaved person is 'I know how you feel.' You don't! Each loss is unique because each person is unique. Certainly similarities exist in the grief experiences of persons who have suffered the same type of loss. When I minister to a woman who has suffered a miscarriage, I always try to find another woman who has had the same misfortune to visit with her. I cannot empathize as much as that woman can.

However, all experiences of loss have in common the general purpose of teaching us dependence on God and His grace. The hymn-writer William Cowper wrote, 'Grief is itself a medicine.'

Symptoms of Grief

When David grieved for his son, he exhibited typical symptoms of grief. He withdrew from society, he lost his appetite, he did not want to discuss it with anyone, he pleaded with God to make it not true.

Grieving individuals often try to deny the reality that causes their hurt; they try to fight the ugly truth. They may withdraw into aloneness and refuse the comfort of others. He may lose all interest in everyday things and people and come to think of life as pointless. They may pray to the Lord to change the reality, or they may turn away from the Lord in anger and disappointment. Telling the hurting person that this is not the way to react is easy, but as Shakespeare put it, 'Everyone can master a grief but he that has it.'

The most common symptom of grief is not mentioned in this particular passage: weeping. When humans grieve, the lachrymal glands in the eyes tend to unloose copious amounts of tears, sometimes without warning or apparent cause. Mourning people often find themselves crying for no apparent reason.

The act of weeping actually provides some relief and healing. Don't tell those who mourn not to cry. Why shouldn't they cry? The apostle Paul declares that Christians do not weep as unbelievers who have no hope, but he does not assert that we should not weep at all. We are supposed to weep – it is beneficial.

Jesus could have laughed when standing beside Lazarus' tomb because He knew that in a few short seconds He would raise Lazarus from the dead and restore him to his grieving family. But instead, He wept. Why? He felt the pain of loss, even though it was only temporary. Crying is the natural reaction for humans, even the perfect divine-human, Jesus Christ.

Withdrawing from other people and refusing to eat for a time are understandable, but not helpful, reactions to grief. Weeping for a while, however, is helpful as well as normal.

Stages of Grief

When Jesus told His disciples, 'Blessed are those who mourn' (Matthew 5:4), He was referring to those who mourn over their sinfulness. They will know the blessing of God because mourning draws us closer to God. Mourning over a loss should likewise result in blessing in our lives by drawing us closer to God. But how?

Human emotions are too complex to follow neat, mechanical procedures. Nevertheless, it is valid and helpful to recognize stages in a normal grief experience, even through the stages may not be separate and clearly distinguished.

1. *Shock*. Our first reaction to loss may be numbness. We may feel psychologically paralyzed. We do not know how to act; we are confused and hurting; we experience anger or fear or both. We may deny the reality of the loss and rebel against accepting the facts.

2. *Acceptance*. We eventually acknowledge the brutal reality. It is no longer a nightmare – it is the way things are. We contemplate the fact that though we are still here, from now on, life will be different.

3. *Feeling the loss*. As we try to carry on with our lives, we are confused and tired, we have little appetite, we sleep poorly, we avoid other people. Sometimes we weep, other times we feel like weeping and nothing happens. We have doubts about the goodness, kindness, and wisdom of God.

4. *Living with it*. We begin to separate the past, which cannot be changed, from the future, which can be affected. We are able to remember the good times associated with the lost person and to re-evaluate our new situation, even making some tentative decisions about the future. We begin to relate to other people more normally.

5. *Renewal*. We begin to find meaning and purpose in the present and future. We renew our commitment to life and to people, becoming involved again in their lives and taking an interest in the external world. Eventually we are able to care about other people and their needs as much as our own.

The process of grief may take some time; it cannot be rushed. It takes longer for some people to recover than for others. Recognizing the stages of grief on paper is not difficult, but in real life, they are not so clear-cut. We may go through the stages in a different order or go through some more than once. As C. S. Lewis said, 'In grief, nothing "stays put". One keeps on emerging from a phase, but it always recurs.' We do not get over grief, we get through grief. The good news is that, as the poet Shelley observed, 'Grief itself is mortal.'

One day in the 1880s, Mary Woods stumbled along the waterfront in Calais, Maine, located near the Canadian border, with a crumpled piece of paper in her hand. The telegram read: 'Emma dead in childbirth. Baby girl alive.' Mary stared into the swirling water, bitterly reviewing her life. Her first-born daughter and her twins had all died of measles in infancy. Her son Charles died at 10 in a freak accident; Ella died at 12; Will died at College, of typhoid fever. Emma had been her consolation – now she too was gone. The churning water whispered to her, 'Come to me.'

Just then, a child's voice said: 'You goin' to jump? I'll jump with you. I'm scared to do it alone.' The girl was clothed in a ragged filthy dress and had the dirtiest face Mary had ever seen. Self-pity vanished and she took the urchin home, washed, fed, and clothed her, and listened to the girl tell her of the other urchins that lived on the streets and in the cellars of Calais. The next day Mary began a new life, a life of rescuing street children, cleaning them up and finding adoptive parents for them. She formed the Calais Benevolent Society, a movement that has since placed millions of children in homes. The cure for Mary's grief and ours is often to be found in helping others worse off than ourselves. Joy and love are feelings that leave no room for grief.

Managing Grief

The right way to handle grief is spiritual, as found through Scripture and prayer. It is also important to take care of the physical, as well as the spiritual aspects of our being.

After describing David's grief over his son's imminent death, the twelfth chapter of 2 Samuel goes on:

On the seventh day the child died. David's servants were afraid to tell him that the child was dead, for they thought, 'While the child was still living we spoke to David, but he would not listen to us. How can we tell him the child is dead? He may do something desperate.'

David noticed that his servants were whispering among themselves and he realized the child was dead. 'Is the child dead?' he asked.

'Yes,' they replied, 'he is dead.'

Then David got up from the ground. After he had washed, put on lotions and changed his clothes, he went into the house of the LORD and worshiped. Then he went to his own house, and at his request they served him food, and he ate.

His servants asked him, 'Why are you acting this way? While the child was alive, you fasted and wept, but now that the child is dead, you get up and eat!'

He answered, 'While the child was alive, I fasted and wept. I thought, "Who knows? The Lord may be gracious to me and let the child live." But now he is dead, why should I fast? Can I bring him back again? I will go to him, but he will not return to me.'

Then David comforted his wife, Bathsheba (verses 18-24).

David reacted to his grief in the right way. He addressed his physical needs and his spiritual needs. 'He washed, put on lotions, and changed his clothes .... they gave him food, and he ate.' A grieving person needs to care for his body, mind, and spirit. Here are some guidelines:

1. Drink plenty of milk, juice, and water – not caffeine or alcohol.

2. Eat a balanced diet – not junk food – even if you don't feel like it.

3. Make yourself rest even if you can't sleep.

4. Make yourself exercise moderately.

5. Do not change your job or house, if at all possible.

6. Arrange for a medical check-up three months after your loss.

7. Talk to friends and family about your loss, even if it hurts.

8. Accept the help of others, even if it is clumsily offered.

9. Find someone else who is hurting and help them a little.

All of these practical things will help you to get through your own loss. Of course, the spiritual aspect of our nature is even more important. The difference between Christians and non-Christians is not that Christians do not feel pain, but that they do not despair. Despair is loss without hope, which is not possible for anyone who understands and believes the gospel of God.

Grief provides a surprising challenge and opportunity for the believer to re-evaluate his commitment to the gospel and to our Lord Himself. We must learn to see present pain in the light of future hope. Jesus Himself sweated in pain in the garden of Gethsemane over the imminent loss of union and communion with His heavenly Father. He overcame His grief by anticipating and focusing on the joy of reunion with His Father. We must do the same.

We learn to do this by meditating on the facts of the gospel and the rich promises of the Word of God. We can experience the comfort David experienced: 'Even though I walk through the valley of the shadow of death, I will fear no evil, for you are with me; your rod and your staff, they comfort me' (Psalm 23:4). David did not deny or suppress the reality of evil and suffering in his life but he overcame it with the reminder that the Lord was his shepherd. Even when we do not feel His presence, He is with us. How do we know? Because God has told us so in His Word. 'Jesus loves me, this I know, for the Bible tells me so.'

The psalmist wrote, 'Precious in the sight of the LORD is the death of His saints' (Psalm 116:15), and the author of Revelation stated, 'Blessed are the dead who die in the Lord ... they will rest from their labors, for their deeds follow them.' To go on and on grieving for the loss of a beloved Christian implies denial of these statements. It is 'far better', as Paul wrote, 'to be with the Lord'.

If the beloved person we miss was not a Christian, we can take comfort and hope in the wisdom and goodness of God and the mystery of His providence, and trust that when we meet the Lord we will understand what we do not and cannot now understand. Mourning reminds us of our total dependence on God to truly understand anything.

We must believe Romans 8:23,35,37: 'We know that in all things God works for the good of those who love Him, who have been called according to His purpose. ... Who shall separate us from the love of Christ? Shall trouble or persecution or famine or nakedness or danger or sword? ... No, in all these things we are more than con-

querors through Him who loved us.' It is often in grief
that we come to really believe and trust these glorious
truths.

In his book, *Trusting God*, Jerry Bridges relates the experience of the hymn-writer John Newton:

'John Newton, author of the hymn Amazing Grace,
watched cancer slowly and painfully kill his wife over a
period of many months. In recounting these days, John
Newton said: 'I believe it was about two or three months
before her death, when I was walking up and down the
room, offering disjointed prayers from a heart torn with
distress, that a thought suddenly struck me, with unusual
force, to this effect – "The promises of God must be true;
surely the Lord will help me, if I am willing to be helped!"
It occurred to me, that we are often led ... (from an undue
regard of our feelings), to indulge that unprofitable grief
which both our duty and our peace require us to resist to
the utmost of our power. I instantly said aloud, "Lord, I
am helpless indeed, in myself, but I hope I am willing,
without reserve, that thou shouldest help me." '[4]

Bridges describes how Newton's prayer was answered
with the remarkable peace that he was subsequently able
to enjoy as he went about his everyday duties. But Newton was helped only because he chose to be helped. Trusting God was an act of his will, and it brought the comfort
of the Holy Spirit. That choice will deliver mourning souls
today from their pit of suffering. Blessed are those who
mourn, for they shall be comforted !

---

4. Jerry Bridges: *Trusting God* (Colorado Springs, Navpress, 1988).

Epilogue

JOY?

Psalm 13

How long, O LORD? Will you forget me forever?
  How long will you hide your face from me?
How long must I wrestle with my thoughts
  and every day have sorrow in my heart?

Look on me and answer, O LORD my God.
  Give light to my eyes, or I will sleep in death;
my enemy will say, 'I have overcome him';
  and my foes will rejoice when I fall.

But I have trusted in your unfailing love;
  my heart shall rejoice in your salvation.
I will sing to the LORD,
  for he has been good to me.

Is there an antidote to the ugly feelings which often lead the Christian into sin? Can we overcome the emotions of fear, depression, anger, hatred, guilt, envy and grief? A few years ago, Bobby McFerrin sang *'Don't worry – Be happy!'* and this catchy little song rocketed to the top of the charts; just as quickly it sank from view. Why? Because it was just so *irritating*! People realized very quickly that simply telling people to stop worrying and just be happy is not only useless advice, it is also annoyingly useless.

The Biblical answer may sound somewhat similar at first glance, but it is in fact fundamentally different. Far from offering glib and superficial advice, the gospel provides a gradual, long-term practical solution. This is found in the gospel portrayal of the Christian life as one of joy, and the child of God as one who is able by the grace of God to rejoice in every one of life's situations.

Now we must understand that joy is not the same as happiness. The pursuit of happiness is a constitutional right which proves to be extremely elusive. Humans seek happiness in power, money, success, sport, the arts, romance, prestige, etc. But the fact is that humans are still unhappy more often than not – because their happiness is based upon events, things, circumstances, which by definition are constantly changing.

If our happiness is dependant on the ever-changing circumstances of life, then obviously we will keep on losing it. To the God-less person, happiness comes from good things happening, and unhappiness comes from bad things happening.

The message of the gospel is that this need not be so:

119

the child of God can have more than mere happiness: he can live a life of joy – whatever is happening around him. And the Bible teaches that this indeed is the will of our Father for His children. Despite our ugly emotions, and in the midst of the events and people that stimulate them, the Christian can and should know joy.

Let us review some of the New Testament teaching.

It is not ambiguous; for example James tells us to 'Count it all joy when you experience various trials' (James 1:2). Without God this is plainly a ridiculous idea.

But Jesus states: 'I have spoken these things to you so that My joy may remain in you, and that your joy may be full' (John 15:11).

Paul describes joy as one of the evidences of the Spirit's indwelling: 'The fruit of the Spirit is love, joy, peace', etc. (Galatians 5:22). And so it is not unrealistic for the apostle to command Christians: 'Rejoice in the Lord. Rejoice in the Lord always. Again I say rejoice!' (Philippians 3:1; 4:4; also 1 Thessalonians 5:16).

Joy is not an elective. It is what distinguishes true Christianity from all man-made religions. Living in God's kingdom is to live in an environment of joy: 'The kingdom of God is not eating and drinking, but righteousness, peace, and joy in the Holy Spirit' (Romans 14:17).

When we ask how this is possible, we notice something immediately in the book of Acts, which records the experiences of the first Christians. Their startling joyfulness, in the midst of cruel persecution, was due to their devotion to the work of God among them – the proclamation of the gospel, the miraculous healing power of God, the love of God manifest in their midst, even the persecutions they experienced – all this was to them a source of continual rejoicing. It confirmed their faith in Christ and it confirmed their own privileged identity as the beloved family of the living God.

They did not pray for the suffering to stop so much as they prayed for the Father to glorify Jesus through their lives and witness (Acts 8:8; 13:52; 15:3; 20:24).

Paul in fact boasts: 'I am exceedingly joyful in all our tribulations' (2 Corinthians 7:4). He does not mean because of, but in the midst of. The cause often is Paul's pleasure in what God is doing in the lives of his converts (Philippians 4:1) or what God is doing through others (Philippians 1:18).

Similarly, John states that 'I have no greater joy than to hear that my children are walking in the truth' (3 John 4). To help them rejoice, he says, he has written this letter to them (1 John 1:4). His fellowship with other believers is also a source of joy to the apostle (2 John 12).

The testimony of the New Testament is that Christians can and should rejoice always, can and should live lives that are characterized by joy; why then, is this so rare these days?

I believe that we have lost sight of the fact that we are called not to seek happiness, but joy. The difference is that happiness is dependant on circumstances, and that it is (literally) self-centered, while joy is finding pleasure in the eternal truths which are above our temporary circumstances, and focusing our desires on Jesus.

Troy, a young man who suffers from manic depression, or bipolar disorder, told me recently that his life had been revolutionized by a remark a preacher made in a recent sermon. The preacher had observed that while it is impossible to find joy *in* some circumstances, it is always possible to find joy *during* those circumstances – joy *in the Lord*. My friend had not until then understood the difference.

This indeed is the key. We are not called to pretend that things are always fine – they are not; life is full of disappointment and pain; we should grieve over our own sin, because it does offend the Lord. *But* – whatever the circumstances may be, the believer can and should find joy in Christ. What that means in practice is that when we feel bad, or low, we must learn to pray that the Holy Spirit will enable us to focus our hearts on the great truths of the gospel; meditate on the greatness and glory of our wonderful God; meditate on the work of Jesus Christ – His life, His death, His resurrection; meditate on the benefits that come to the believer through the ministry of the Spirit; meditate on the destiny of believers who will hear the voice of Jesus say to them one day soon: 'Enter into the joy of the Lord' (Matthew 25:21, 23).

This is how, when our ugly feelings spoil our peace of mind and tempt us to sin, we can overcome them by expelling them; they are expelled from our hearts by renewed realization of the glory of God, the love of Jesus, and the destiny of God's people. Even while our emotions rage, our minds can subdue our feelings by covering them with the joy of the Lord. 'The joy of the Lord is my strength' said David. We can know this too.

Make a joyful shout to God, all the earth!
  Sing out the honor of His name
  Make His praise glorious
Say to God, 'How awesome are your works!'
(Psalm 66:1-3)

We began this book by observing how the Old Testament psalms reflect and express the many emotions that believers experience today; this is true of the feeling of joy also, but what is especially helpful to us is to observe how often this emotion is the expression of a *conscious decision* by the author. This is how the writer gradually overcame his negative emotions; with the added clarity and fullness of the New testament gospel we must learn to do the same.

Consider such psalms as these and meditate on them:

'My heart *shall rejoice* in your salvation
I *will sing* to the LORD' (Psalm 13:5, 6).

'I *will be glad and rejoice* in your mercy,
For you have considered my trouble' (Psalm 31:7).

'My soul *will be joyful* in the LORD;
It *shall rejoice* in His salvation' (Psalm 35:9).

'Make a joyful shout to the LORD, all you lands!
  Serve the LORD with gladness.
  Come before His presence with singing.
Know that the LORD, He is God' (Psalm 100:2).

'This is the day that the LORD has made;
We *will rejoice* and be glad in it' (Psalm 118:24).